# Thirteen Steps to Better Writing

## Joan D. Berbrich, Ph.D.

**Amsco books by Joan D. Berbrich**

Fifteen Steps to Better Writing
Laugh Your Way Through Grammar:
    Blue, Yellow, Green, Tan, Orange
Macbeth: A Resource Book
101 Ways to Learn Vocabulary
Reading Around the World
Reading Today
Thirteen Steps to Better Writing
Wide World of Words
Writing About Amusing Things
Writing About Curious Things
Writing About Fascinating Things
Writing About People
Writing Creatively
Writing Logically
Writing Practically

**Amsco School Publications, Inc.**
315 Hudson Street / New York, N.Y. 10013

When ordering this book, please specify either **R 435 W** or
THIRTEEN STEPS TO BETTER WRITING

ISBN 0-87720-666-X

# Dear Student:

If you walk *step-by-step*, you can cover a mile, a dozen miles, even a hundred miles without panicking.

If you put together bicycle parts *step-by-step*, you will end with a bicycle—instead of a mess of unrecognized nuts and bolts.

If you learn to operate a computer *step-by-step*, you will soon become an expert, able to make the machine perform wonders.

The key to learning anything difficult is—tackle the task *step-by-step*.

That is why this text is set up *step-by-step*. There are only THIR-TEEN steps—and you can easily handle THIRTEEN steps, can't you?

Writing *is* difficult. It is a civilized skill, and a complex one. And it is an essential one in our modern world. Without it, you cannot truly think. Without it, you cannot adequately express your own ideas. Without it, you are like an 8-cylinder engine limping along on four cylinders.

So what do you do? You learn to write—and to write well—and you do it *step-by-step*.

You begin with the **parts of speech** (six steps), and as you learn them, you *use* them—and your writing begins to improve dramatically.

You go on to the **various kinds of sentences** (three steps), and as you master them, you *use* them—and your writing improves still more.

You continue with **variations in sentence structure** (four steps), and as you comprehend them, you *use* them—and your writing gains in power and clarity.

Before you know it, *you* will be a writer—not a professional writer, but a writer just the same. You will be able to influence others—through your writing. You will be able to communicate with others—through your writing. You will be able to clarify and stengthen your thinking—through your writing.

And you can accomplish all this by working your way *step-by-step* through the thirteen steps to better writing!

\* \* \* \* \*

Naturally you learn faster (and more effectively) when you are having fun, and interesting subject matter makes that possible.

*Which would tempt you to travel?*

"Germany at Low Cost"

OR

"Germany on a Beer Budget"

*Which would hold your interest?*

> . . . information about fungus

OR

> . . . information about a Pancake Race

*Which would you remember longer?*

> . . . a paragraph about Dick and Jane going to the store

OR

> . . . a paragraph about a *real* Banana Olympics

To capture your interest, to hold your interest, and to help you learn, we have used in this text sentences and paragraphs based on fascinating news items, curious trivia, and amusing facts. As you master these basic writing techniques *step-by-step*, you will also be chuckling at a pig that danced for Louis XI, at a sour-pickle flavored chewing gum, and at the reason we shake hands instead of rubbing noses. And as you chuckle, you will learn to write and to enjoy writing.

∗　∗　∗　∗　∗

*BONUS TECHNIQUE*. Start your own file of fascinating information that you read or hear about. Then, when you write, *use* these. Imagine how an essay on playing the piano can be brightened by a sentence or two about a proficient, piano-playing pig! Imagine how an essay on "first jobs" can be enlivened by an anecdote about an actor-director who started life as a cleaner of bird cages! Use trivia, and you will enjoy writing—and you will be confident that your reader will enjoy reading. So . . . enjoy!

∗　∗　∗　∗　∗

*MARGINALIA*. Don't miss the MARGINALIA! (**Marginalia:** notes in the margins of a book.) The cartoons should tickle your eyes, the riddles your mind, and the reminders your memory. They will help you to understand and remember what you are studying. So notice . . . relish . . . chuckle . . . and LEARN!

*Cordially yours,*

*Joan D. Berbrich*

# CONTENTS

---

## Parts of Speech

---

STEP I.    USE SPECIFIC NOUNS    *1*

     1. Specific Nouns: Learn Them!    *3*

     2. Specific Nouns: Use Them!    *7*

     3. Specific Nouns: Use Them in *Your* Writing!    *12*

STEP II.    USE SPECIFIC VERBS    *16*

     4. Specific Verbs: Learn Them!    *18*

     5. Specific Verbs: Use Them!    *22*

     6. Specific Verbs: Use Them in *Your* Writing!    *26*

STEP III.    USE APT ADJECTIVES    *31*

     7. Apt Adjectives: Learn Them!    *33*

     8. Apt Adjectives: Use Them!    *38*

     9. Apt Adjectives: Use Them in *Your* Writing!    *42*

     Writing Time—I    *46*

STEP IV.    USE AGILE ADVERBS    *49*

     10. Agile Adverbs: Learn Them!    *51*

     11. Agile Adverbs: Use Them!    *55*

     12. Agile Adverbs: Use Them in *Your* Writing!    *59*

STEP V.    USE PERSONAL PRONOUNS CORRECTLY    *64*

     13. Personal Pronouns: Learn Them!    *66*

     14. Personal Pronouns: Use Them!    *69*

     15. Personal Pronouns: Use Them in *Your* Writing!    *75*

STEP VI.    USE PURPOSEFUL PREPOSITIONS    *81*

     16. Purposeful Prepositions: Learn Them!    *83*

     17. Purposeful Prepositions: Use Them!    *88*

     18. Purposeful Prepositions: Use Them in *Your* Writing! *93*

     Writing Time—II    *96*

# Various Kinds of Sentences

STEP VII.  USE ALL FOUR TYPES OF SENTENCES   *101*

   19. Four Types of Sentences: Learn Them!   *103*

   20. Four Types of Sentences: Use Them!   *108*

   21. Four Types of Sentences: Use Them in *Your* Writing!   *113*


STEP VIII.  USE COMPOUND SENTENCES   *118*

   22. Compound Sentences: Learn Them!   *120*

   23. Compound Sentences: Use Them!   *124*

   24. Compound Sentences: Use Them in *Your* Writing!   *128*


STEP IX.  USE COMPLEX SENTENCES   *132*

   25. Complex Sentences: Learn Them!   *134*

   26. Complex Sentences: Use Them!   *138*

   27. Complex Sentences: Use Them in *Your* Writing!   *144*

   Writing Time—III   *148*

# Variations in Sentence Structure

STEP X.  USE APPOSITIVES   *152*

   28. Appositives: Learn Them!   *154*

   29. Appositives: Use Them!   *159*

   30. Appositives: Use Them in *Your* Writing!   *165*


STEP XI.  USE PARALLEL STRUCTURE   *172*

   31. Parallel Structure: Learn It!   *174*

   32. Parallel Structure: Use It!   *179*

   33. Parallel Structure: Use It in *Your* Writing!   *185*

**STEP XII.**   **USE VERBALS**   *191*

    **34.** Verbals: Learn Them!   *193*

    **35.** Verbals: Use Them!   *200*

    **36.** Verbals: Use Them in *Your* Writing!   *206*

**STEP XIII.**   **USE SENTENCE COMBINING**   *210*

    **37.** Combining Sentences: Nursery Level   *212*

    **38.** Combining Sentences: Junior Level   *216*

    **39.** Combining Sentences: Senior Level   *218*

    **40.** Combining Sentences: Use Them in *Your* Writing!   *223*

    Writing Time—IV   *226*

---

# "Put It All Together . . ."

---

**PORTFOLIO I.**   **SNAKES**   *233*

    **1.** Finding Answers   *235*

    **2.** Writing a Report   *236*

    **3.** Writing a Friendly Letter   *239*

    **4.** Writing a Fable   *241*

**PORTFOLIO II.**   **NAMES**   *242*

    **5.** Writing a Filler   *244*

    **6.** Writing a Book   *246*

    **7.** Writing a Friendly Letter   *249*

    **8.** Writing a Report   *250*

**PORTFOLIO III.**   **MOVIES**   *252*

    **9.** Writing a Business Letter   *254*

    **10.** Writing a Report   *257*

    **11.** Writing a Persuasive Letter   *259*

    **Index**   *261*

A

CARDINAL

AND A

RACCOON,

A

MILLIONAIRE

AND A

BURGLAR

**USE**

**SPECIFIC**

**NOUNS**

THE FIRST STEP TO BETTER WRITING is to use **specific nouns** whenever possible. They add spice to your sentences, pep to your paragraphs, and excitement to your essays!

> "There's gold in them there hills!"
>
> . . . NOW THAT'S BETTER THAN . . .
>
> "There's a mineral in them there places."
>
> *Note:* Of course, "them there" is ungrammatical. *Never* use it—unless you are quoting a gold miner!

How do you find **specific nouns?** Become a miner. Dig in your memory and in your reference books; watch for their "glitter" when you read.

# 1

## SPECIFIC NOUNS

## LEARN THEM!

███████████████████████████████████████████

All right, you gold prospector! You have a burro and a shovel, a sack (to carry your gold nuggets in), and some dried jerky to chew on. You're ready to start mining for gold . . . or rather, for specific nouns.

**SPECIFIC: naming a particular person, place, or thing.**

Your brain is already loaded with specific nouns. You just forget they're there when you start writing. Let's look at a typical student-written sentence.

> For dinner, I had meat, potatoes, and vegetables.

Dull, dull, dull . . .

**Meat** is too general. **Roast beef** is more specific; so is **chicken.** Think of three more *specific* meats and list them below.

_____

**Potatoes** is too general. **French fries** is more specific; so is **potatoes au gratin.** List three more specific kinds of potatoes.

_____

**Vegetables** is too general. **Asparagus** is more specific; so is **zucchini.** List three more specific vegetables.

_____

Now rewrite the original sentence substituting specific nouns for general nouns:

For dinner, I had _____, _____, and _____.

Isn't that a better, more descriptive sentence than the original one? Of course it is—because it uses *specific nouns.*

**A. BECOME AWARE**

A noun is a name
  Of Anne and Paul,
  Of Lucille Ball,
    Jack Benny, too.

A noun is a name
  Of Boise and Maine,
  Of Toledo, Spain,
    And Kalamazoo.

A noun is a name
  Of house and home,
  Of hair and comb,
    Of sock and shoe.

A noun is a name.

3

Back to gold mining. In each of the following sentences, one word is printed in **boldface** (dark type). That word is a general noun. After each sentence, list *three* specific nouns or noun phrases that would improve the writing.

**1.** Little Amy likes **candy.** (One example: lollipops.)

_____

**2.** Before going out into the storm, Melissa put on **warm clothing.** (Example: a fur-lined jacket.)

_____

**3.** Terry is reading a **book.** (Example: *Star Wars.*)

_____

**4.** Twelve-year-old Benjy is watching a **television program.** (Example: "Little House on the Prairie.")

_____

**5.** Jake has the **equipment** he needs to play baseball. (Example: a glove.)

_____

Now you are asked to dig deeper still for specific nouns.

**1.** Find specific nouns that name people or things that you hate or fear. (Examples: ghosts—snobs—nightmares.) Find *six* more.

_____

_____

**2.** Find specific nouns that name the kinds of buildings in which people live. (Examples: hut—castle.) Find *six* more.

_____

_____

This is a word game you can play to increase your knowledge of specific nouns. Just follow the alphabet and find a specific noun that begins with each letter for each category. To get you started, we've filled in a few squares, starting with *anorak*, a hooded jacket or coat. (Don't expect to fill *every* square! When you have finished, give yourself 2 points for each correct insertion. Then add up your score: 60 points = *good*, 80 points = *superior*, 100 points = *outstanding*.)

| | CLOTHING | ANIMALS | TREES | FLOWERS |
|---|---|---|---|---|
| A | *anorak* | | | |
| B | | *baboon* | | |
| C | | | *chestnut* | |
| D | | | | *daisy* |
| E | | | | |
| F | | | | |
| G | | | | |
| H | | | | |
| I | | | | |
| J | | | | |
| K | | | | |
| L | | | | |
| M | | | | |
| N | | | | |
| O | | | | |
| P | | | | |
| Q | | | | |
| R | | | | |
| S | | | | |
| T | | | | |
| U | | | | |
| V | | | | |
| W | | | | |
| X | | | | |
| Y | | | | |
| Z | | | | |

Have you ever browsed through a dictionary? It's a fascinating experience! Begin by checking a dictionary to find definitions for the following specific nouns—all the result of a quick browsing expedition.

1. collywobbles: _____

2. donnybrook: _____

3. ignoramus: _____

4. braggart: _____

5. homily: _____

Continue by doing some browsing of your own. (*Browse:* to look over casually; to skim.) Find two unusual nouns that capture your interest. Write them and their definitions below.

6. _____ : _____

7. _____ : _____

Next make these new nouns your own by using them. Place one of the first five in each of the following sentences.

8. He's a(n) _____, always talking about how great he is.

9. Whenever I get home late, my father launches into a twenty-minute _____.

10. Sitting in the waiting room, she had the _____.

11. Don't let what he says bother you; he's a(n) _____ _____.

12. The debate between the Democrats and the Republicans turned into a fierce _____ .

Finally, write two original sentences, using the two specific nouns that you "discovered."

13. _____

14. _____

# 2

# SPECIFIC NOUNS

## USE THEM!

If you have ever used a camera, you know that if the focusing is off, your picture will be blurred; if the focusing is exactly right, your picture will be sharp and clear. Specific nouns work the same way: with them, your sentences turn into vivid pictures.

**A. BE SPECIFIC!**

Try it!

| | |
|---|---|
| *Don't say:* | "a bird" |
| *Do say:* | "a cardinal" or "an eagle" |

| | |
|---|---|
| *Don't say:* | "an animal" |
| *Do say:* | "a raccoon" or "a grizzly" |

Your turn . . . Copy each of the following sentences, replacing each *general* noun (boldfaced) with a *specific*. Be dramatic!

1.  In the jungle, he came face to face with a full-grown **animal.**

    _____

    _____

2.  Having just won a million dollars, she raced downtown to buy herself a **car.**

    _____

    _____

3.  He dreamed of traveling in foreign lands: of having breakfast in **one country,** lunch in **another country,** and dinner in **still another country.**

    _____

    _____

    _____

**4.** For breakfast, she ate **cereal** smothered with **fruit.**

_____

_____

**5.** Feeling depressed, he turned on the television and watched a **comedy show.**

_____

_____

Do specific nouns make a difference?

B. BE SPECIFIC!

| | |
|---|---|
| _Don't say:_ | The **man** walked down the **street.** |
| _Do say:_ | The **millionaire** walked down **Fifth Avenue.** |

| | |
|---|---|
| _Don't say:_ | The **man** walked down the **street.** |
| _Do say:_ | The **tramp** walked down the **alley.** |

Notice the power of the specific nouns. **Millionaire** or **tramp** tells us a good deal more than **man; Fifth Avenue** evokes a far sharper picture than **street.**

Your turn . . . Write _five_ new versions of the basic sentence below. Create these versions by replacing the two boldfaced _general_ nouns with various _specific_ nouns. The basic sentence:

The **woman** entered the **building.**

> _Ask yourself: What kind of woman? What is her occupation? In what activity is she engaged?_
>
> _Next, ask yourself: Into what kind of building would this particular woman be going? Draw a logical relationship between the woman and the building._
>
> Example: The **lawyer** entered the **courthouse.**

**1.** _____

**2.** _____

**3.** _____

**4.** _____

**5.** _____

Work a little magic again by copying each sentence *after* you have replaced the boldfaced general nouns with specific nouns.

1. The **animal** clawed the **tree.**

   _____

2. The **bird** ate a(n) **insect.**

   _____

3. The **athlete** did some **exercises.**

   _____

4. The **child** threw a(n) **object.**

   _____

5. The **musician** played a(n) **song.**

   _____

Before you continue, read each pair of sentences, the original and the revised. Which of the two tells you more? Which helps you to *see* what is happening?

A paragraph comes to your desk. Read it.

> Up in the tree, a bird sang, its voice warm and melodious. Nearby, an animal crouched, watching the bird. Emotion made the animal's eyes glitter. Stealthily it began to slink forward, body to the ground. It was only a little distance from the bird when another animal dashed toward it from the next yard. As the first animal fled, the bird flew down and perched confidently on the second animal's head.

It's all right, but it doesn't *zing*. You wonder: if the general nouns were changed to specific nouns, would that make a difference? Try it with the boldfaced words below . . . tackling one sentence at a time.

1. Up in the **tree,** a **bird** sang, its voice warm and melodious.

   a. What kind of tree? Choose an interesting one.  a _____

   b. What kind of bird? Remember: it must have a melodious song.  b _____

```
TREES

elm
maple
weeping willow
oak
apple
white birch
pine
```

9

2. Nearby, an **animal** crouched, watching the **bird.**

    **c.** What kind of animal? (Be logical!)      c _____

    **d.** For **bird,** see question *b.*      d _____

3. **Emotion** made the **animal's** eyes glitter.

    **e.** What specific emotion (love, hate, fear, greed) probably made the animal's eyes glitter?      e _____

    **f.** For **animal,** see question *c.*      f _____

4. Stealthily it began to slink forward, **body** to the ground.

    **g.** What part of the body would be close to the ground when an animal slinks?      g _____

5. It was only **a little distance** from the **bird** when **another animal** dashed toward it from the next yard.

    **h.** Exactly how far away? How many feet?      h _____

    **i.** For **bird,** see question *b.*      i _____

    **j.** What kind of animal? It must be capable of frightening the first animal.      j _____

6. As the **first animal** fled, the **bird** flew down and perched confidently on the **second animal's** head.

**k.** For **first animal,** see
question *c*.                    k _____

**l.** For **bird,** see question
*b*.                    l _____

**m.** For **second animal,** see
question *j*.                    m _____


Now copy on the lines below the revised paragraph with specific nouns replacing general ones. (Remember to indent the first line of this paragraph.)

_____

_____

_____

_____

_____

_____

_____

_____

_____

_____

_____

_____

_____

_____

Finally, read both paragraphs, the original (page 9) and the revised. Well, what is your decision? Do specific nouns make a difference?

# 3

## SPECIFIC NOUNS

## USE THEM IN <u>YOUR</u> WRITING!

Now that you have become aware of specific nouns, you should find it easier—and more fun—to write. Tackle the following assignments. (Remember: if your memory needs jogging as you seek specific nouns, review pages 3 through 11.)

**A.** It is your birthday, and you are being treated to your favorite dinner. Write a paragraph describing it. Use as many specific nouns as you can and underline them. (Before you begin, read the example below.)

---

It was my birthday, and there on the table was my very favorite dinner. I stared greedily before digging in. There were *zucchini boats*, dark green and glittering, stuffed with *chopped meat* and *rice* and *tomatoes*. There was *corn on the cob*, drenched in *butter*, sparkling with *salt crystals*. And there was my *cake*, a *fiesta* of *whipped cream* and sweet juicy *strawberries*.

---

The first two introductory sentences have been provided. *You* finish the paragraph.

It was my birthday, and there on the table was my very favorite dinner. I stared greedily before digging in. There were _____

_____

_____

_____

_____

_____

_____

_____

> *You just organized a paragraph by starting with a generalization (the first sentence) and developing it with supporting details. Easy, wasn't it? This is a good way to organize a paragraph. Remember it!*

**B.** You and a friend are stranded in a cabin near the North Pole. It's twenty below and snowing hard. Your friend volunteers to go for help. He piles on his own clothing plus some of yours. Describe his appearance as he starts out the door. Use plenty of specific nouns. For suggestions, see page 5. (*Organize the paragraph by moving from a generalization [sentence 3 below] to supporting details.*)

Max opened the door cautiously. Even so, the wind almost blew it off its hinges and the snow tore in. He stood, looking rather like a child's teddy bear, in _____

_____

_____

_____

**C.** Write a descriptive paragraph on any topic you choose. Some possibilities:

> (*a*) an alley between two buildings
> (*b*) a park *or* playground
> (*c*) a city street *or* a country road
> (*d*) a person who dresses in unusual fashion

## PROCEDURE

*Step 1:* Choose a topic. Which of the above topics (*a*, *b*, *c*, or *d*) can you *see* most clearly in your mind? With which are you most familiar? Select one and write it below.

_____

*Step 2:* Think about your topic. Create a picture and fill it with details.

EXAMPLES:

(*a*) Is *your* alley filled with dented trash cans and half-starved cats, with puddles of dirty water and a sleeping tramp?

(*b*) Is *your* park or playground bright with white swings and red begonias, with slides and monkey bars, with a gazebo and green benches?

(c) Is *your* country road lined with birch trees and oaks, with wide pastures populated by grazing cows, with occasional cornfields in which the corn is five feet high, tassels fluttering in the breeze?

(d) Is *your* oddly-dressed creature a pop singer in a black suit spattered with rhinestones, with a derby from the 1930s painted red, with cowboy boots covered with tiny bells?

Create *your* picture, complete with details. Write details below.

_____

_____

_____

_____

_____

_____

_____

_____

_____

*Step 3:* Develop a generalization based on your choice of details.

EXAMPLES:

(a) Between the Curran Building and the public library lies a twisting alley which the respectable carefully ignore.

(b) Like a refreshing oasis in a stone-grey city is Kids Park, a colorful playground filled with fascinating and challenging contraptions.

(c) Travel a few miles along Route 24 in late August, and you will find yourself in a natural paradise.

(d) Most young people are horrified at the thought of wearing something "not in style," but this pop singer sets her own style—and does it with a flair!

*Your* generalization . . .

_____

_____

_____

Step 4: Now write your descriptive paragraph, using many strong specific nouns. Make your paragraph as vivid, as sharp and clear, as a good picture!

_____

_____

_____

_____

_____

_____

_____

_____

_____

_____

_____

_____

*Organize your paragraph by moving from your generalization, or general statement, to supporting details.*

Now read the paragraph you just wrote. Are you pleased with it? Is it exciting, fun to read? Check it. Are there any general nouns that should be replaced with specific ones? If there are, change them now. (Sometimes you will *choose* to keep a general noun. Fine—as long as you are doing it by choice!)

WRITING TECHNIQUE

# 1

**The use of specific nouns can improve your writing tremendously. Remember this. Become aware of specific nouns in the writing of others. <u>Use</u> them in your own writing.**

WALK:

TRAMP,

MARCH,

TRUDGE,

PLOD,

GALLOP,

STRUT,

AMBLE,

SAUNTER

**USE**

**SPECIFIC**

**VERBS**

THE SECOND STEP TO BETTER WRITING is to use **specific verbs**—preferably **active** ones. They make your writing **gallop** and **soar**—rather than **creep** and **crawl!**

> *Brandishing* his cane, the old man *fought off* the snarling dogs.
>
> . . . A BIT BETTER THAN . . .
>
> *Waving* his cane, the old man *held off* the snarling dogs.

How do you find **specific verbs?** The same way you found specific nouns: dig in your memory and in reference books; be alert for vivid verbs when you read.

# 4

## SPECIFIC VERBS
## LEARN THEM!

You see vivid verbs in books and in magazines; you hear them on television and at football games. The trick is—to become aware of them *and* to use them in your own writing.

Let's start by teasing your memory to unearth some of the vivid verbs you already know.

A. BECOME AWARE

1.  **EAT**—everybody likes to eat. But the *right* verb actually describes the way someone eats. Start with the sentence: "Jesse **ate** his supper." If Jesse was in a hurry, it would be more accurate to write . . . "Jesse **gulped** his supper."

    Try filling in the missing verbs below—with *vivid* verbs that indicate *specific* ways of eating. (We've provided a few key letters as well as the number of missing letters.)

    **a.** Jesse SW _ _ _ _ _ _ D his supper.
    (He ate fast, without chewing.)

    **b.** Jesse D _ V _ _ _ _ D his supper.
    (He was starved.)

    **c.** Jesse P _ _ K _ D at his supper.
    (He wasn't hungry.)

    **d.** Jesse N _ B _ _ _ D at his supper.
    (He wasn't hungry.)

    **e.** Jesse G _ _ B _ _ D up his supper.
    (He ate fast and without manners.)

Do you see? You surely knew at least three of these specific verbs—but have you ever used them in your writing? You should.

2. **FOLLOW** is a common verb, but not a strong one.

   The sheriff **followed** the cattle thief.

Fill in the missing verbs.

   **a.** The sheriff P _ _ S _ _ D the cattle thief.

   (tried to overtake him)

   **b.** The sheriff T _ _ _ L _ D the cattle thief.

   (went more slowly looking for prints and other clues)

   **c.** The sheriff C _ _ S _ D the cattle thief.

   (followed him rapidly)

   **d.** The sheriff S _ _ _ _ W _ D the cattle thief.

   (followed him closely but didn't let himself be seen)

3. **WALK**—another common verb.

   The clown **walked** into the arena.

Fill in the missing verbs.

   **a.** The clown M _ _ C _ _ D into the arena.

   (moved with a rhythmic stride)

   **b.** The clown A _ B _ _ D into the arena.

   (moved in a leisurely way)

   **c.** The clown P _ _ D _ _ D into the arena.

   (moved heavily and slowly)

   **d.** The clown S _ _ _ T _ _ D into the arena.

   (moved proudly, almost boastfully)

Mine that memory of yours and try to find *specific*, *vivid verbs* for the blanks in the following clusters.

1. You can **PLAY** an instrument, or

   B _ _ T a drum,

   S _ _ _ M a guitar,

   T _ _ E up a fiddle, or

   B _ _ W a trumpet.

2. She **PUT** the toy clown on the table.

   PL — — — —

   S — —

   P — — CH — —

   P — S — T — — N — —

3. He **FROWNED** when he saw his report card.

   S _ _ W _ _ _

   P _ _ T _ _

   SN _ _ L _ _

4. She **HELD UP** the flag.

   R _ _ _ E _

   L _ _ T _ _

   H _ _ ST _ _

   BR _ _ D _ _ H _ _

5. He **CRIED** when he broke his leg.

   W _ P _

   S _ _ B _ _

   WH _ _ P _ _ _ _ _

   M _ _ N _ _

6. She **TOOK** the lollipop from the baby.

   G _ _ B _ _ _

   SN _ _ _ H _ _

   S _ _ Z _ _

   C _ P _ _ _ _ _

7. He **SAW** a ghost.

   R _ C _ _ _ _ Z _ _

   N _ T _ _ _ _ _

   SP _ _ _

   OB _ _ _ V _ _

8. You can **STAND ABOVE** your enemies, or you can

   R _ _ E above them,

   H _ V _ R above them,

   L _ _ M above them.

9. He **TOOK BACK** his bike from the bully.

   R _ C _ P _ _ _ _ _

   R _ T _ _ _ V _ _

   R _ C _ V _ _ _ _

   SN _ _ C _ _ _ back

10. She **SHOUTED** when she saw the dinosaur.

    R _ _ R _ _

    Y _ _ _ _ _ _

    B _ L _ _ W _ _

    SC _ _ _ M _ _

It's dictionary browsing time again. Check a dictionary to find definitions for the following specific verbs.

**1.** shuttlecock: _____

**2.** yammer: _____

**3.** bludgeon: _____

**4.** zoom: _____

**5.** taunt: _____

Continue by doing some browsing of your own. Find two unusual specific verbs that you think you may be able to use some time. Write them and their definitions below.

**6.** _____ : _____

**7.** _____ : _____

Next make these new verbs your own by using them. Place one of the first five verbs in each of the following sentences.

**8.** Abigail _____ on and on, unaware that Lucy had already left the room.

**9.** Sales of flying saucers _____ sharply right after the Martian invasion.

**10.** "We're on the verge of bankruptcy," said the president. "Let's _____ a few ideas and try to find a way to save ourselves."

**11.** She _____ her little brother until he had a temper tantrum.

**12.** In a panic, Pedro _____ the mosquito with an oar.

Finally, write two original sentences, using the two specific verbs that you "discovered."

**13.** _____

**14.** _____

21

# 5

## SPECIFIC VERBS
## USE THEM!

Dull verbs make dull writing . . . and dull reading.

Vivid, action-packed verbs turn dull writing into exciting reading
. . . as you will soon see.

Replace the dull verbs in the sentences below with vivid, action-
packed verbs. Remember: your goal is to provide details about *how*
someone is doing something and to do this with one well-chosen
verb. (Glance back at Chapter 4, pages 18–21, if you need ideas.)

EXAMPLE:   The ballerina **entered** the theater.

REVISION:   The ballerina **danced** into the theater.

**A. BE SPECIFIC!**

1.  The cardinal **ate** a caterpillar.                                1 _____

2.  The police **followed** the robbers.                              2 _____

3.  The guitarist **played** a folk song.                            3 _____

4.  The burglar **cried** when he was hand-
    cuffed.                                                          4 _____

5.  My friend **talked** about the movie
    until I was ready to scream.                                     5 _____

6.  For six months, Jeremy **watched** the
    behavior of the ants in the ant village.                        6 _____

7.  The detective **followed** the suspect
    for three days without being spotted.                           7 _____

8.  Without a clear destination, Lorrie
    **walked** along the path near the river.                        8 _____

9.  Unable to land, the helicopter **stayed**
    above them and dropped packages of
    food.                                                          9 _____

10. The parrot **sat** on its swinging rod
    shouting, ''I told you so!''                                   10 _____

---●---

**A verb is a word
That runs and pounces,
Jumps and bounces—
Shows action, you see,
Buzzing like a bee.**

---●---

B. WORK A LITTLE MAGIC

Wave your magic wand and transform the following drab sentences into exciting ones, each of which tells a story. Do this by changing general nouns to specific nouns and general verbs to specific verbs.

EXAMPLE: The **man saw** an **animal.**

REVISION: The **prisoner spied** a **bloodhound.**

**1.** The **child hit** the **dog.**

_____

**2.** The **animal ate** the **food.**

_____

**3.** At midnight, the **man played** a drum and **walked** around the **building.**

_____

**4.** The **person took** an **object** from the counter and **left.**

_____

**5.** The zoo seemed melancholy as **some animals cried, some other animals cried,** and **some other animals cried.**

_____

_____

> **If your teacher's eyes
> you wish to light,
> Use the verbs
> that tell it right.**

C. SAY IT AGAIN!

Here's your next challenge. Start with the general verb **say** (past tense: **said**). All that **say** tells us is that someone spoke words. For example, consider this sentence:

"I'll go with you," she **said.**

Was the speaker happy or sad? Excited or bored? A more specific verb would give the answer.

"I'll go with you," she **sobbed.**

(_Now we know she's unhappy, emotionally upset, weeping._)

"I'll go with you," she **lectured.**

(_This time we know she's alert, possibly protective, and suspicious of your reason for going._)

Find as many specific verbs as you can to replace **said** in the basic sentence: "I'll go with you," she **said**. Consult your memory, and—if that doesn't work—check one of these reference books:

**THESAURUS:** a book of words and their synonyms.

**SYNONYM:** a word that has the same or nearly the same meaning as another word.

Roget's *Thesaurus*
Any good book of synonyms
Any good dictionary

Try to find at least a dozen synonyms or near-synonyms for the verb **said**. List them.

_____  _____  _____

_____  _____  _____

_____  _____  _____

_____  _____  _____

This time the paragraph on your desk describes the meeting of a human being and a legendary monster. Read it.

**D. PLAY THE PROOFREADER**

> Only half conscious, I **saw** for the first time the Abominable Snowman. He **stood** above me. He **frowned**. He **held up** one huge arm like a club.
>
> "Grr!" he **said**.
>
> "Grr!" I **said**.
>
> He **took** my baseball cap and **put** it on his own gargantuan head. Now I really had a problem. Pride ordered me to **take back** my cap. Prudence suggested otherwise. Prudence won.
>
> "It's all yours," I **said** finally.

This little story could be a good deal more exciting if the bold-faced general verbs were replaced by specific ones. Do it, keeping in mind that you want to convey the fear of the human and the bigness and roughness of the monster. (If you need help, glance back at Chapter 4, pages 18–21.)

When you have made all the suggested changes, copy the revised paragraph below.

_____

_____

_____

_____

_____

_____

_____

_____

_____

_____

_____

_____

_____

_____

_____

_____

Now read both the original and revised stories. Can you see the difference?

# 6

## SPECIFIC VERBS

## USE THEM IN <u>YOUR</u> WRITING!

Meet the following challenges—by using vivid, action-packed verbs as you write. Find them in your memory, or in a dictionary.

**A.** Think about a race—any kind of race. It may be a footrace held during gym class; or a marathon; or a motorcycle race. It may even be a race between competing frogs or turtles! Decide the kind of race you will describe. Then *see* it in your mind. See the contestants line up, start, run. Find good verbs to describe the action you are viewing in your mind. Before you begin, read the example below.

Notice that the paragraph starts with details . . . then ends with a general statement.

> A small green toad, a garter snake, a cockroach, and a mouse *jostled* impatiently at the starting line, restrained by the firm fingers of their owners. As the whistle *blew*, the fingers *flicked* upward—and the race was on! The toad *leaped* twice, then stopped. The cockroach was *distracted* by a crumb of cake, and the mouse by its own tail. The garter snake *slithered* ahead. Finished with its crumb, the cockroach, chased by the mouse, *skittered* around the unmoving toad, while the snake *twisted* itself, slowly, almost reluctantly, across the finish line. A roar went up from a dozen juvenile throats. It was all over! The annual Funny Foursome Race in Looneyville, U.S.A., had been won by the garter snake!

*First Auto Race in U.S.*

When?  1895

Where?  Chicago

Who won?  Frank Duryea

Winner's average speed?
7-1/2 m.p.h.

*Your turn:*  Write a brief description of an unusual race, starting with a barrage of details and ending with a general statement about the race and the winner.

<table>
<tr><td>WORDS TO<br>DESCRIBE<br>COMPETITION</td></tr>
<tr><td>argue</td></tr>
<tr><td>fury</td></tr>
<tr><td>triumph</td></tr>
<tr><td>quarrel</td></tr>
<tr><td>hostile</td></tr>
<tr><td>conflict</td></tr>
<tr><td>opponent</td></tr>
<tr><td>dispute</td></tr>
<tr><td>struggle</td></tr>
<tr><td>threaten</td></tr>
<tr><td>aggressive</td></tr>
<tr><td>challenge</td></tr>
<tr><td>rival</td></tr>
<tr><td>oppose</td></tr>
<tr><td>brawl</td></tr>
</table>

_____
_____
_____
_____
_____
_____
_____
_____
_____
_____
_____
_____
_____
_____
_____
_____
_____
_____
_____
_____
_____

*In Chapter 3 (page 12) you organized a paragraph by starting with a generalization and then adding supporting details. You just did the reverse: you started with the details and moved to a generalization. Both methods of organization are useful. Remember them!*

**B.** Recall a conflict between any two people or any two groups of people. Some possibilities:

        (a) a verbal battle between two people

        (b) a fistfight or wrestling bout

        (c) a competition in which two people compete through speeches, drawings, models, etc.

        (d) an athletic contest

## PROCEDURE:

*Step 1:* **Choose a topic.** Which of the above can you *see* most clearly in your mind? With which are you most familiar? Select one and write it below.

_____

_____

*Step 2:* **Now put your memory to work.** Recall the words said in the conflict you have chosen. Recall the tone of voice used. Recall any gestures made. Recall body movements. Recall facial expressions. List below as many details as you can—all dealing with the two people or two groups of people in conflict.

_____

_____

_____

_____

_____

_____

_____

_____

_____

_____

_____

_____

_____

*Step 3:* **Finally describe the conflict,** using strong action-packed verbs to make the reader see it, too. (Organize the descriptive paragraph by giving the details first, and then moving on to a generalization.)

_____

_____

_____

_____

_____

_____

_____

_____

_____

_____

_____

_____

_____

_____

_____

_____

_____

_____

**c.** You made a one-minute telephone call to your cousin who lives a thousand miles away. Just before the minute was up, your cousin asked: "What have you been doing with yourself?" You decide to answer in a short, amusing note. Select one chore you have often done: raking leaves, washing windows, taking care of a baby sister, going shopping—any chore at all. Describe the steps in doing this chore, using strong nouns and vivid verbs. (The format has been provided below. *Organization: start with a generalization (sentence 2 of the letter); then add supporting details.*)

---

April 3, 19 — —

Dear _____,

    You asked what I have been doing with myself. Well, I've been _____, that's what!

_____

_____

_____

_____

_____

_____

_____

_____

_____

    As you can see, I've been keeping busy, in a <u>most</u> exciting way. I hope your life is half as interesting!

        As ever,

        _____

---

*WRITING TECHNIQUE*

# 2 ▬▬▬▬▬▬▬▬▬▬▬▬▬▬▬▬▬

**Specific verbs—like specific nouns—add color to your writing. Use them. You'll find Writing Technique #2 fun—and effective!**

# A WHITE, FLOPPY-EARED BEAGLE

## USE APT ADJECTIVES

THE THIRD STEP TO BETTER WRITING is to use ***apt adjectives***—
adjectives that describe something or someone *exactly*.
With apt adjectives, you can make a reader see a **fuzzy,
crawly** caterpillar or a **fierce, teeth-baring** Doberman!

> *"Obesity is really widespread."*  (Joseph Kern II)
>
> . . . CLEVER, AND SO MUCH BETTER THAN. . .
>
> *"Obesity is really very common."*

You find apt adjectives just as you found specific nouns
and verbs: in your memory and in reference books, in your
reading and in your listening (to people, TV, radio, etc.).

Watch for **apt adjectives.** Remember them. Use them.

# 7

## APT ADJECTIVES
## LEARN THEM!

**Apt adjectives** are everywhere: in magazines and newspapers, in books, on radio, in conversation, even on television! Just tune in—store in your memory—and use.

Start by really looking at the titles of television programs. Producers want short, easy-to-remember titles: often just an adjective and a noun.

*Sometimes they use <u>alliteration</u>: the repetition of the initial sound of two or more words:*
    *Hogan's Heroes—Sesame Street*

*Sometimes they use a <u>pun</u>: a play on words:*
    *Knight (Night) Rider*

Using the clues above, combine the adjectives in Column I with the nouns in Column II to create punchy, easy-to-remember TV titles. The titles you create may be ones actually used on TV or may be original ones of your own.

| *Column I* | | *Column II* |
|---|---|---|
| Tic Tac | _____ | Feud |
| Star | _____ | Boat |
| Candid | _____ | Zone |
| Family | _____ | Woman |
| Different | _____ | People |
| Twilight | _____ | Camera |
| Romper | _____ | Search |
| Love | _____ | Room |
| Real | _____ | Dough |
| Wonder | _____ | Strokes |

**33**

Before going on, name one TV title that . . .

. . . uses alliteration _____

. . . is based on a pun _____

. . . in your opinion is especially APT. _____

## B. BECOME AWARE— OTHER MEDIA

Part of "becoming aware" of **apt adjectives** is understanding *why* a particular adjective, or adjective-noun combination, is APT. The following examples have been culled from newspapers and magazines and should challenge your brain!

EXAMPLE: BURRO BONANZA (a headline of a story about burros air-lifted from the Grand Canyon and offered to buyers for $50 a piece)

ANALYSIS: **Bonanza** is a good noun because it indicates the buyer is getting a real bargain. **Burro** is an apt adjective because it describes exactly the kind of bonanza. Also, the two words are alliterative and therefore catchy.

YOUR TURN:

1. DELTA DREAM VACATION (an ad): Why not "fantasy vacation" or "exciting vacation"? Why is **dream** an apt adjective?

   _____

   _____

2. ANTI-POLLUTION EFFORTS LAG IN SMOGGY PRAGUE (a headline): Why **smoggy?**

   _____

   _____

3. AN OLD TRAIN PROVIDES PLATFORM FOR 'NEW' IDEAS ( a headline): Generally, **old** is too common to be apt; but in this headline it is exactly right. Why?

   _____

   _____

4. GERMANY ON A BEER BUDGET (an ad): Why not "champagne budget"? At whom is the ad aimed? Why is the ad "catchy"?

   _____

   _____

34

**5.** A TINY, FLIGHTLESS BIRD STALLS U.S. STRATEGIC AIR COMMAND (a headline): Would the headline be just as effective if the bird were described as a "huge, winged bird"? Why not?

_____

_____

---

Adjectives are **_modifiers:_** they limit the nouns they modify. Consider the noun _hair_.

_Red_ hair: the adjective _red_ limits _hair_. It makes clear the hair is not brown, nor black, or white—only _red_.

_Curly_ hair: the hair is not straight.

_Long_ hair: the hair is not short.

An adjective **modifier** limits and makes more specific the noun it modifies.

---

C. PROBE YOUR MEMORY

Suppose you want to describe an APPLE. You might start . . .

a **red** apple

Urged to be more specific, you might add . . .

a **round, red** apple, **tasty, firm,** and **smelling good**

Better, much better, because you have used your various senses to help describe the apple. But a little thought would unearth more specific, more APT adjectives to modify the noun _apple_.

**RED** (rosy, scarlet, rust-colored, crimson)
**ROUND** (circular, orb-shaped, oval, rotund, bulbous)
**TASTY** (sweet, tart, tangy, luscious, mouth-watering)
**FIRM** (crunchy, crisp, brittle, solid)
**SMELLING GOOD** (sweet-smelling, pungent, fragrant, scented)

Now it is possible to write a sharper, more vivid description:

a **bulbous crimson** apple, **tart, crunchy,** and **pungent**

or—if you find that a bit heavy, you might compromise . . .

a **round, rosy** apple, **tart** and **crunchy** and **smelling good**

The trick lies in teaching your mind to search your memory for possible alternative adjectives—for _exact_ adjectives. Ready to try it on your own?

1. Describe an ORANGE. First, list three adjectives for each category. For guidance, study the adjectives used to describe an apple on the previous page. Or create your own adjectives.

Color: _____ _____ _____

Shape: _____ _____ _____

Taste: _____ _____ _____

Texture: _____ _____ _____

Smell: _____ _____ _____

Now select *one* adjective from each category and describe an ORANGE:

_____

_____

2. Describe a PENCIL.

Color: _____ _____ _____

Shape: _____ _____ _____

Taste: _____ _____ _____

Texture: _____ _____ _____

Smell: _____ _____ _____

Again, select *one* adjective from each category and describe a PENCIL:

_____

_____

When is a pencil like a good joke?

When it has a point.

3. This time simply find APT adjectives to replace the boldfaced adjectives in the following sentences. (Try to find at least *five* for each sentence.)

a. A **shiny** new car pulled into our driveway.

_____ _____ _____

_____ _____ _____

b. The video game emitted a series of **loud** sounds.

_____ _____ _____

_____ _____ _____

c. He walked slowly down the **dirty** street.

_____ _____ _____

_____ _____ _____

36

Wander through the pages of a dictionary to find definitions for the following adjectives:

1. belligerent: _____

2. gargantuan: _____

3. ominous: _____

4. exultant: _____

5. candid: _____

There are 490,000 words in the English language, plus 300,000 technical terms.

Continue by doing some browsing of your own. Find two adjectives that appeal to you. Write them and their definitions below.

6. _____ : _____

7. _____ : _____

Next make these adjectives your own by using them. Place one of the first five adjectives in each of the following sentences.

8. A(n) _____ smile trembled on the lips of the new "Miss America."

9. "Oh, stop posing! I'm taking only _____ shots today!"

10. Because the weather was _____, we cancelled plans for a picnic.

11. The bush monster, _____ and hostile, terrified the earliest colonists on Mars.

12. The two neighbors, equally _____, faced each other with clenched fists and snarling expressions.

Finally write two original sentences, using the two specific adjectives that you "discovered."

13. _____

14. _____

# 8

## APT ADJECTIVES
## USE THEM!

Adjectives can turn a **dull, leaden** day into a **splendiferous** one; they can turn a **stringent** teacher into a **forbearing** one. So it behooves you to *use* apt adjectives!

**A. ADJECTIVE ARSENAL**

An *arsenal* is a place where weapons are stored. For a writer, words are weapons. Probe the arsenal in your mind for apt adjectives that will be useful in the following situation.

You are riding your bicycle and you spot a strange dog. Make the reader see the dog.

First change **dog** to a specific noun.

Is it a *St. Bernard* or a *poodle*, a *collie* or a *cocker spaniel*?

Then add two adjectives.

Is it *large, huge, small, petite, gargantuan*?

Is it *brown, black, white,* or *red*?

Is it *snarling, growling,* or *barking*?

You should end with a phrase something like this: "a **huge, snarling** greyhound" or "a **white, floppy-eared** beagle" (recognize Snoopy?).

Develop your own phrase (two adjectives + a specific noun) for the dog you are describing.

_____

**B. A SAFARI SIGHT**

This time you are a photographer on a jungle safari. You've just taken a nap. As you open your eyes, you see—just six feet away–an "animal." Decide: what kind of animal? (We'll take the *aardvark*. You take any animal except the aardvark.) Next add two adjectives. Our descriptive phrase: "a **six-foot-long, belligerent** aardvark." Your descriptive phrase?

_____

Consider this sentence: "The viewer turned off the TV." Reading it, we have no idea *why* the viewer turned it off. The right (*apt*) adjective can suggest the cause.

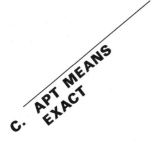

*Situation:*    The viewer loves football, and a football game was preempted by a soap opera.

*Basic Sentence:*    The _____ viewer turned off the TV.

*Apt Adjective:*    **furious** or **infuriated**

Provide an adjective that would be appropriate for each of the following situations. Some possibilities:

| | |
|---|---|
| **exhausted** | **nervous** |
| **faint-hearted** | **skeptical** |
| **fearful** | **terrified** |
| **guilt-stricken** | **timid** |
| **impatient** | **weary** |

1. *Situation:*  The viewer has been watching TV for six hours without a break.

   "The _____ viewer turned off the TV."

2. *Situation:*  The viewer has just heard an announcement that the two superpowers are on the brink of nuclear war.

   "The _____ viewer turned off the TV."

3. *Situation:*  The viewer has just watched a commercial claiming that anyone who drinks Sizzling Soda will live to be a hundred.

   "The _____ viewer turned off the TV."

4. *Situation:*  The viewer has been watching a program that he or she is not permitted to watch and hears a parent enter the room.

   "The _____ viewer turned off the TV."

5. *Situation:*  The viewer has been watching a live show in which trapeze artists work without a net.

   "The _____ viewer turned off the TV."

Sometimes one adjective is better than another because it is less common, because it builds a sharper picture. In each of the following sentences, underline the adjective in parentheses that you think is more effective.

1. The (**hot, broiling**) sun scorched their bodies.

2. They scurried for cover when they heard the (**ominous, loud**) roar of the approaching tornado.

3. The (**exultant, happy**) surfer shouted as she reached the crest of the highest wave.

4. After the hailstorm, the farmer stared miserably at his (**battered, damaged**) corn crop.

5. The tiny Toyota collided with a (**huge, large**) moving van.

As a writer, you will sometimes want to use startling adjective-noun combinations: combinations that have seldom—if ever—been used before.

Consider the adjective **blazing.** Writers have often used blazing fires and blazing eyes. How about trying it with "book"? A blazing book—now there's a thought . . . a book that sets you on fire! You've heard of a soggy cracker or soggy bread. How about a soggy smile (from a weepy child), or soggy thinking (from a lazy student)? Get it?

Be as far-out as you like, but make sense at the same time. Create *three* unforgettable adjective-noun combinations. To help you get started we'll provide a list of adjectives, some common, some uncommon.

**ADJECTIVE-NOUN COMBINATIONS**

bowlegged picnic table
soda-pop giggle
tailgating elephants
squiggly laughter
baby-blanket clouds
corrugated frown
dazzling asterisks

| | | |
|---|---|---|
| spicy | rickety | tender |
| tame | thundering | blazing |
| soggy | crisp | yawning |

_____

_____

_____

You have just found on your desk a report of a young man's vacation. It's interesting, but the writer used **nice** eight times! Your job is to replace each **nice** with a more exact, more colorful adjective. First read the paragraph.

F. PLAY THE PROOFREADER

> Jim had a **nice** time in Arizona. He met Jerry, a **nice** fellow his own age, and together they had some **nice** experiences. They rode mules down the Grand Canyon, feeling like early explorers. That was **nice**. They took a five-day Navajo tour and were thrilled by the **nice** sand paintings and the **nice** tribal dances. They spent a day at Colored Rock Canyon and were stunned by the **nice** colors created by the sun beating down on the weird terrain. At the end of the trip, Jim declared that he had had a **nice** time.

To help you get started, we are providing a few adjectives, but try to add some of your own.

| | | |
|---|---|---|
| amusing | fascinating | marvelous |
| breathtaking | friendly | splendid |
| exciting | intricate | vivid |
| fantastic | magnificent | |

When you have decided which adjectives to use to replace each **nice**, copy the revised paragraph below.

_____

_____

_____

_____

_____

_____

_____

_____

_____

_____

_____

_____

_____

Now read both the original and the revised reports. You decide—do adjectives make a difference?

# 9

## APT ADJECTIVES

## USE THEM IN <u>YOUR</u> WRITING!

Here are three writing assignments that will make you explore your mind to find **apt adjectives.** Write as concretely, as vividly, as possible.

**A.** Describe some common object—but *do not name it*. Use exactly the right adjectives (and specific nouns and verbs) to convey the sight, the smell, the taste, the sound, the texture. When you have finished, swap papers and see if readers can guess correctly the object you described. (*Before you begin, read the example that follows.*)

> To pursue my favorite pastime, I need an object that may be any size but is usually about nine inches high and six inches wide. The *hard* exterior may be *red*, or *green*, or *blue* (or any other color), but the *soft* interior is almost always *white* and *black*. It gives off a *tangy* scent, disliked by many people but loved by me. Sometimes I let my fingers caress the exterior, anticipating the delights that lie within; but always I soon turn to the interior, eager for the joys and the sorrows, the wisdom and the adventures, the moments of tragedy and the sparkling flashes of humor. It is my window to the future, my sailing sloop to the past, and my companion in the present. IT IS A _____ . (See page 44 for the answer.)

*Paragraph organization: start with descriptive*  *details; end with a generalization.*

*Your turn . . .*

_____

_____

_____

_____

_____

_____

_____

_____

_____

_____

_____

_____

_____

_____

_____

**B.** Reread the **nice** paragraph—*your* revision on page 41. Inspired by this and using it as a pattern, write a brief report of a teenager's sightseeing in your state. Be specific—both in naming the places visited and in describing these places and the teenager's reactions. (*Paragraph organization: a generalization, then supporting details, then back to the generalization.*)

---------------

**WORTH SEEING?**

**Museums**
**Historic Buildings**
**Amusement Parks**
**Natural Wonders (moun-**
    **tains, lakes, etc.)**
**Restaurants**
**Plays, Operas**
**Sports Activities**
**Festivals**
**Special Shops or Malls**
**Cruises, Mule Trips, etc.**

---------------

_____

_____

_____

_____

_____

_____

_____

_____

_____

_____

_____

The answer to the description of a certain object on page 42 is, of course, a BOOK.

**C.** Your aunt sent you a birthday gift, and you are planning to write a thank-you note (of course!). BE SPECIFIC!

> DON'T SAY: "Thank you for the **nice** scarf."
> DO SAY: "Thank you for that **dynamic crimson** scarf."
> DON'T SAY: "It keeps me warm."
> DO SAY: "It makes me **glow** even in November gales."

Think of your aunt reading the note and write it so *she* will glow—and perhaps send you another gift next year. Check the format for a friendly note on page 30. (*Organization: start with a generalization, move to supporting details, and—if you like—end with the generalization.*)

_____
(date)

Dear _____,

_____
_____
_____
_____
_____
_____
_____
_____
_____
_____
_____
_____
_____

_____,
(closing)

_____
(signature)

# 3

Apt adjectives add spice to your writing. They make it come alive; they make it sing. But—like spices—apt adjectives should be used sparingly. A little goes a long way.

# WRITING TIME—I

Given *any* reason at all, people will do the weirdest things. What's more, they'll do them every year and brag about them!

Practice your writing skills by penning paragraphs about the following three "weird activities"—all annual celebrations staged somewhere in the U.S. Don't try to include *all* the information; select only what you want. But *do* make the descriptions alive and amusing. (*Organize each of the three paragraphs using the generalization to supporting details method.*)

**A. SNOWMAN BURNING CEREMONY**

*Where and when:* Sault Ste. Marie, Michigan; March 20th every year.

*Purpose:* To say good-bye to winter and to welcome spring.

*Activities:* Reading of poems that pan winter and praise spring.
Crowd-cheering of a seven-foot paper snowman.
Burning of the paper snowman to the tune of "I Don't Want to Set the World on Fire."

_____

_____

_____

_____

_____

_____

_____

_____

**B. MULE DAYS CELEBRATION**

*Where and when:* Columbia, Tennessee, in April every year.

*Purpose:* To celebrate the mule.

*Activities:* Mule parade; mule competitions; mule auction.
"Most outrageous lie" contest, open to adults and kids.
Tobacco-spitting contest; checkers tournament.
Pancake breakfast.

_____

_____

_____

_____

_____

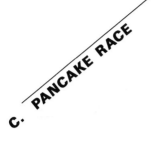

**C. PANCAKE RACE**

*Where and when:* Liberal, Kansas; Shrove Tuesday (preceding Ash Wednesday) every year.

*Purpose:* To prepare for Lent by making pancakes, thus using up any stored fat.

*Activities:* A 415-yard race through main streets of town (open only to married women, over sixteen). Each woman carries a pancake in a skillet and flips it from time to time. Anyone who drops a pancake is dropped from the race.

*Added note:* This race has been run since 1951, but it's been a tradition in Olney, England, for centuries. Today the women of Kansas race against the women of Olney, England, and honor the *international* winner.

_____

_____

_____

_____

_____

_____

Before you continue, go back and reread your three paragraphs. Did you use strong specific nouns, vivid verbs, and apt adjectives? If you didn't, do some revising now.

**D. LET'S CELEBRATE**

It's time to put them all together. We've provided a title: "Let's Celebrate!" You . . .

. . . Write an introductory paragraph; *or* use the first paragraph of this chapter, page 46 ("Given . . . about them!"), as your introductory paragraph.

. . . Write paragraphs 2, 3, and 4 based on the paragraphs you wrote in exercises A, B, and C above (and remember to indent each paragraph).

. . . Write a concluding paragraph (brief) something like this:

> *Why* do people do crazy things in
> public? Maybe to attract tourists . . .
> maybe to make money . . . but most
> likely just to have fun!

Ready? Put it all together on the next page.

Remember to use:

specific nouns

vivid verbs

apt adjectives

_____
_____
_____
_____
_____
_____
_____
_____
_____
_____
_____
_____
_____
_____
_____
_____
_____
_____
_____
_____
_____
_____
_____
_____
_____
_____
_____
_____
_____
_____

There you have it—a report, written by *you*, that is fun to read!
(That's every writer's dream.) What's more, it was probably fun to
write, too. Wasn't it?

HE'S

GRINNING

(GRIMLY,

HAPPILY,

SADLY)

USE

AGILE

ADVERBS

THE FOURTH STEP TO BETTER WRITING is to use **agile adverbs**—adverbs that describe *when* or *where* or *how* something is done. With agile adverbs, you can make an athlete run **frantically**, or **proudly**, or **heavily**—and think of the different pictures evoked by those three adverbs!

> *"This log must weigh a thousand pounds,"* the lumberjack said <u>heavily</u>.
>
> (If you're not grinning, check the Tom Swifties on pages 53, 54.)

Watch for **agile adverbs**. Remember them. Use them.

# 10

## AGILE ADVERBS

## LEARN THEM!

What an adjective does for a noun, an **adverb** does for a verb.

Remember: An **adjective** answers the question *what kind of?* about a noun.

> What kind of person? A **tall** person, a **fat** person, a **happy** person, a **pretty** person.

All are adjectives, describing the noun "person."

An **adverb** usually answers the question *how?* about a verb.

> How does she walk? She walks **fast**, she walks **rapidly**, she walks **steadily**, she walks **firmly**. How does he talk? He talks **pleasantly**, he talks **swiftly**, he talks **softly**, he talks **grimly**.

All are adverbs, describing the verbs "walk" and "talk."

**A. BECOME AWARE**

1. Someone says, "The youth is smiling"—and you wonder: *how?*

He is smiling **grimly**, or **happily**, or **merrily**, or **fiendishly**.

Notice that each adverb gives a different meaning to the verb "smiling." You try it now. Someone says: "Melissa is driving"— and you wonder: *how?* Develop a cluster of *four* adverbs that describe *how* Melissa is driving.

a. Melissa is driving_____.

b. Melissa is driving_____.

c. Melissa is driving_____.

d. Melissa is driving_____.

**2.** As you have seen, most adverbs answer the question *how?* But a few answer the questions *when?* or *where?* or *how often?* Read the following examples carefully.

---

"When are you going to Mexico?"
"I'm driving **there tomorrow**."

Driving *where?* **There. There** answers the question *where?* and therefore is an adverb.

Driving *when?* **Tomorrow. Tomorrow** answers the question *when?* and therefore is an adverb.

---

"How often do you ski and surf?"
"I **often** ski, but I **seldom** surf."

Ski *how often?* **Often. Often** answers the question *how often?* and therefore is an adverb.

Surf *how often?* **Seldom. Seldom** answers the question *how often?* and therefore is an adverb.

---

Many adverbs that answer *when?* or *where?* or *how often?* do *not* end in "-ly." For example, all of the following *may* be used as adverbs.

| | | | |
|---|---|---|---|
| fast | later | now | soon |
| hard | long | often | straight |
| here | loud | seldom | there |
| late | low | slow | tight |

You try it now. Suggest an adverb (from the list above) that will complete each of the following sentences.

**a.** Maxine said she would mow the lawn_____.

(meaning—*in a few minutes*)

**b.** Ali said he would mow the lawn_____.

(meaning—*in several hours*)

**c.** He is always in trouble because he drives too_____.

**d.** Your science book is _____, not in school.

**e.** Said one acrobat to another: "Hold_____."

52

**3.** Adverbs are versatile: in addition to describing verbs, they can also describe adjectives and other adverbs.

---

**Adjectives**, remember, are modifiers: they limit and make specific the nouns they modify. *Red* hair—*curly* hair—*long* hair.

**Adverbs**, too, are modifiers: they limit and make specific the verbs, adjectives, or other adverbs they modify.

*Example*: The story is **tremendously interesting**.

**Interesting** is an adjective, modifying—and describing—the noun "story."

**Tremendously** is an adverb, modifying—and describing—the adjective "interesting."

*Another example:* He spoke **rather bitterly**.

**Bitterly** is an adverb, modifying—and describing—the verb "spoke."

**Rather** is an adverb, modifying—and describing—the adverb "bitterly."

---

*Practice.* In the sentences below, circle each adverb and then draw an arrow from the adverb to the word it modifies. (The modified word may be a verb, adjective, or another adverb.)

**a.** Luis was extremely angry.

**b.** They talked nostalgically of their school days.

**c.** "She is a sweet child," the kindergarten teacher said gently.

**d.** As the rain clouds grew larger, he painted more rapidly.

**e.** Kim was very shy.

**B. ADVERB ANTICS— TOM SWIFTIES**

It is important to recognize adverbs, but it is far more important to use them effectively. You can sharpen your adverb awareness and have fun at the same time by playing the "Tom Swifties" game. It works like this.

"My pencil needs sharpening," she said p _ _ _ _ _ _ _ _ _ _ .

Now a pencil that needs sharpening no longer has a point, so the correct adverb (of course!) is *pointlessly*.

"My pencil needs sharpening," she said pointlessly.

Here's another:

"You make me boil," the cook said **h** _ _ _ _ .

> Boiling suggests something hot, and the cook is obviously angry, so the logical adverb (you guessed it!) is *hotly*.

"You make me boil," the cook said hotly.

To help you master "Tom Swifties," we're giving you the first letter of the correct adverb and blanks that tell you how many more letters are in the adverb. Good luck—you'll need it!

1. "I didn't go to school today," she said **a** _ _ _ _ _ _ _ .

2. "You need an operation," the surgeon said **c** _ _ _ _ _ _ _ .

3. "All my beautiful vases shattered!" the glassblower said **b** _ _ _ _ _ _ .

4. "This cream has turned," the housewife said **s** _ _ _ _ _ .

5. "I prefer flying to driving," the pilot said **a** _ _ _ _ _ .

6. "Unposed pictures are usually better than posed pictures," the photographer said **c** _ _ _ _ _ _ _ .

7. "There is no moon tonight," he said **d** _ _ _ _ _ .

8. "The score is 20 to 4, our favor," he said **w** _ _ _ _ _ _ _ .

9. "Give me that knife!" she said **s** _ _ _ _ _ _ .

10. "Of course our pickles are sour," the storeowner said **t** _ _ _ _ _ .

Now make up three Tom Swifties of your own—and rest assured that **adverbs** will then be **firmly, surely, indelibly, permanently** impressed on your brain!

11. _____

_____

12. _____

_____

13. _____

_____

# 11

## AGILE ADVERBS
## USE THEM!

Adverbs are **marvelously** graphic and **vigorously** active. Master them and they will help you to write **vividly**.

**A. ARRANGING ADVERBS**

Spruce up the following sentences by inserting on each blank an adverb from the list below. Use each adverb only once and arrange carefully so that every sentence makes sense.

| | |
|---|---|
| cleverly | fiendishly |
| desperately | greedily |
| eerily | painfully |
| electronically | skillfully |
| enthusiastically | wearily |

1. Jeremy tramped _____ along the path.

2. In the mountains, the loon cried _____, terrifying the campers.

3. The seals barked _____, each receiving as a reward a bit of fish.

4. Using a computer, a student from Maine chatted _____ _____ with a student from Oregon.

5. "The only way out of this cave is past me," the monster snarled _____.

(The adverb does *not* have to follow the verb. It can be somewhere else in the sentence.)

6. The lion _____ devoured its prey.

7. _____ she fought her way out of the trap.

55

**8.** He steered the boat _____

past the menacing sea serpent.

**9.** As the vultures gathered, she moved her broken arm _____

_____ in an attempt to throw stones at them.

**10.** The clown used makeup _____

to make herself look like a Cabbage Patch doll.

**B. MEET THE STARS**

Top entertainers both talk and are talked about. In each quotation below, you are offered a choice of two adverbs. Choose the better one: the one that is more exact, more colorful, and more rhythmical. (More rhythmical: the one that *sounds* better.)

**1.** "Let's face it. I've (**at last, finally**) arrived." (*Angela Lansbury*)

**2.** "When you are young, there is (**always, sometimes**) someone around to spit on your dreams." (*Frank Sinatra*)

**3.** "The days in my life that stand out most (**clearly, vividly**) are the days I've learned something." (*Lucille Ball*)

**4.** "Laughter is a frown turned (**around, upside down**)." (*Walt Disney*)

**5.** "Berlioz says nothing in his music, but he says it (**magnificently, well**)." (*James G. Huneker*)

**C. ON BEHALF OF WEATHER FORECASTERS**

This "weather writer" has lost her adverbs. Help—by inserting the exactly right adverb in each blank. (Find them in your memory. They're right there—just dig a little!)

"Flurries," the Weather Bureau had _____

predicted. And at first it seemed they were right.

At two p.m. the snow began falling _____.

By three, our world was covered with a blanket of snow, but by four, the blanket had become a heavy quilt.

Flurries?

Homebound traffic inched _____

through deep snowdrifts, while drivers swore _____

at the Weather Bureau and its erroneous prediction. By midnight, three feet of snow had fallen. Cars lay _____ in ditches.

Dangling _____ , live electric wires spluttered.

Flurries. . .

Notice that this paragraph is made more effective by the use of repetition. The first "Flurries" simply makes a statement. The second ("Flurries?") asks a skeptical question. The third and last ("Flurries . . .") makes a weary, rather bitter comment. Keep this small technique in mind when *you* write: a dose of repetition can brighten your writing.

## D. BAN "VERY"!

Many people have a tendency to overuse the adverb "very." Everything and everyone is **very** sweet, **very** good, **very** bad, or **very** smart. Any word that is overused loses some of its power. Today's writer looks for substitutes: substitutes that are more exact, more colorful, more agile. That's *your* job in the sentences below: replace each **very** with a better adverb. (Suggestions are given in parentheses.)

1. While his team fell apart, the coach managed to remain **very** calm.
   (**seriously, furiously, exceedingly**)

   1 _____

2. The monster wore a(n) **very** familiar cap . . . mine!
   (**astonishingly, prudently, truly**)

   2 _____

3. Because of its nationwide tour, the rock 'n' roll group earned a(n) **very** large salary last year.
   (**cruelly, absolutely, incredibly**)

   3 _____

4. Nina thought her brother was **very** silly when he tried to break the record for sitting on a chimney.
   (**abundantly, monstrously, remarkably**)

   4 _____

5. The small visiting alien was **very** shocked when it learned that humans often waged war among themselves.
   (**bitterly, cleverly, decidedly**)

   5 _____

A paragraph on your desk is intriguing but not as lively as it might be. First read it.

When Mark Parker caught a **very** ordinary black bass, he didn't guess what lay ahead. At home he began cleaning the bass. Suddenly he felt a **very** sharp pain. **Very** annoyed, he withdrew his finger from the fish's mouth and drew out—along with the finger—a **very** angry water moccasin. Shortly before being caught, the bass must have swallowed the snake, tail-first. The snake, upset by all the unusual activity, simply did what snakes do best: it bit! One can predict that, in the future, Mark Parker will be **very** cautious any time he starts to clean a just-caught fish.

**Would you believe this story is _true_?**

All right. It's editing time. Select an adverb to replace each **very.** You will find many suggestions in pages 49 through 57. Then copy the revised paragraph below. (Remember: if you use an adverb beginning with a vowel [_a, e, i, o,_ or _u_], change the preceding "a" to "an.")

_____

_____

_____

_____

_____

_____

_____

_____

_____

_____

_____

_____

_____

_____

Now read both the original and the revised paragraphs. Isn't _your_ revised paragraph sharper? More interesting? Adverbs _do_ make a difference!

# 12

## AGILE ADVERBS

## USE THEM IN YOUR WRITING!

Here are three writing assignments to test your skill in using *agile adverbs* (as well as *apt adjectives*, *specific nouns*, and *vivid verbs*!)

**A.** An autobiography–the story of one's own life—can be dull, but it can be made to sparkle with a little imagination. Select *three* related events from your life . . . perhaps three times during your life when you showed a bit of heroism—or terrified your parents—or even made money in an unusual way. Think back over your life. Find three such related incidents and list them below.

_____

_____

_____

You now have the raw material for a tiny but fascinating autobiography. First read the pocket autobiography below.

---

On July 4, 1970, the little town of Mesa, Vermont, was huddling *helplessly* under a thunderstorm when it was hit by a bolt of lightning—**Me!** *Actually* the town *barely* noticed my birth, but it did notice me ten years later. At 4 a.m. on my tenth birthday I climbed the flagpole in front of the Village Hall with three small cans of paint dangling from my belt. A flagpole **should** be red, white, and blue, shouldn't it? At twelve, I awakened the town to Independence Day by *fiercely* tolling the church bell. . . at midnight. At fourteen, I shot a year's savings on some spectacular fireworks. As the rockets danced *gracefully* over Mesa, people looked at me with a thoughtful respect. . . and some awe. At fifteen—well, I have an intriguing idea. . .

---

Ready to write your own? Start with your birth and relate it in some way to the three events you have already selected. Next describe these three events *in the order in which they occurred*. It will help if you specify your age at the time of each event. Use sharp adjectives and adverbs, vivid nouns and verbs. Finally—end with a look ahead.

Your turn. . .

_____

_____

_____

_____

_____

_____

_____

_____

_____

_____

_____

_____

_____

_____

_____

_____

_____

_____

_____

_____

*You just organized a paragraph in a new way: you organized it <u>chronologically</u>. This means you started with the earliest event (your birth) and proceeded—according to time—to three later events. You can use the chronological approach to describe someone else's life, to give the history of a place or object, or to give directions for a process.*

**B.** This time write a brief, meaningful history of **The Fourth of July.**

**1.** First read the notes below.

—The Continental Congress adopted the "Declaration of Independence" on July 4, 1776, in Philadelphia, then the nation's capital. The Declaration of Independence proclaimed our independence from Great Britain.

—In the mid-nineteenth century, people celebrated the Fourth with picnics. They had watermelon-eating contests, potato races, and patriotic speeches.

—The British were occupying Philadelphia on July 4, 1778, but other areas celebrated the new holiday.

—In the 1950s, fireworks were banned in many states.

—In 1777, in Philadelphia, the Fourth of July was celebrated with sermons, bonfires, speeches, and fireworks.

—The term, the "Glorious Fourth," was first used in Philadelphia in 1777.

—Today, July 4th is celebrated in _____

(insert the name of your town or city) with _____

_____

**2.** Organize the notes above *chronologically.* Place a #1 before the event that occurred first, #2 before the event that occurred second, etc.

ODD...

**President Thomas Jefferson died on July 4.**

**President John Adams died on July 4.**

**President James Monroe died on July 4.**

**3.** Select from the previous notes (except #1) *three* events or statements that are related in some way. (Examples: the use of fireworks on the Fourth; or methods of celebrating the Fourth.) Write these three items below, *in chronological order*.

_____

_____

_____

**4.** Now relate item #1 to your major idea or angle and write an introductory sentence. Then continue writing, describing briefly each of the three events you chose. (Use chronological order, of course, and use the nouns and verbs, adjectives and adverbs that are *exactly* right.)

_____

_____

_____

_____

_____

_____

_____

_____

_____

_____

_____

_____

_____

_____

_____

_____

_____

_____

_____

A *fish story* is simply an extravagant or incredible tale. The origin of the phrase probably lies in the tendency of anglers (people who like to fish) to tell ''whoppers'' about the fish that got away. Today, the fish story can be about fish--or about anything else. Reread the fish story on page 58. Then concoct one of your own. It may be a true experience (the one on page 58 *is* true); a story you have heard; or a completely fictitious one. Organize your story chronologically. Write it on scrap paper; then return to this page.

\*    \*    \*    \*

Now check your fish story. Are the nouns specific? The verbs action-packed? The adjectives exact and vivid? The adverbs powerful? If not, make revisions. Copy the revised fish story below.

_____

_____

_____

_____

_____

_____

_____

_____

_____

_____

_____

_____

_____

_____

_____

_____

_____

_____

**WRITING TECHNIQUE**

**4** ━━━━━━━━━━━━━━━━━━━━━━━━

Agile adverbs are an effective aid to powerful writing. Use them sparingly, but use them well.

IT'S
ALL
IN
THE
POINT
OF
VIEW

USE
PERSONAL
PRONOUNS
CORRECTLY

THE FIFTH STEP TO BETTER WRITING is to use **personal pronouns** effectively. Proof? Consider the difference between ...

> "*I* am boxing. The big money and all the popularity of this sport is because of me." (*Muhammad Ali*)
>
> *He* is boxing. The big money and all the popularity of this sport is because of him.

Only Muhammad Ali could get away with the first statement; but wouldn't it have been more effective—even for Ali—if someone else had said it *about him*?

The difference between "I" and "he" is only one little letter; yet that letter makes all the difference ... to our **point of view**.

"*I* am boxing."

# 13

## PERSONAL PRONOUNS

## LEARN THEM!

A **personal pronoun** takes the place of a person's name.

Personal pronouns are short words, each no longer than six letters and each a single syllable.

Personal pronouns are few in number (only 26).

Personal pronouns are as colorless as air. Compare with specific nouns and verbs, apt adjectives and agile adverbs.

First review your knowledge of personal pronouns by studying the chart below.

**A. THE PERSONAL PRONOUNS**

|  | *Nominative* | *Objective* | *Possessive* |
|---|---|---|---|
| *1st person:* | I or we | me or us | my, mine, our, ours |
| *2nd person:* | you | you | your, yours |
| *3rd person:* | he, she, it, or they | him, her, it, or them | his, her, hers, its, or their, theirs |

Don't let the grammatical terms bother you.

The **first** person denotes the *speaker*;

the **second** person, the *person spoken to*;

the **third** person, the *person spoken about*.

**Nominative** simply means that these particular pronouns are used as the *subjects* of verbs: as the doers of action.

> **I** cleaned the robot.
> **We** cleaned the robot.
> **You** cleaned the robot.
> **He** cleaned the robot.
> **She** cleaned the robot.
> **It** cleaned the robot.
> **They** cleaned the robot.

**Objective** simply means that these particular pronouns are used as the *objects* of verbs: as the receivers of action.

> The robot cleaned **me** or **us**.
> The robot cleaned **you**.
> The robot cleaned **him** or **her** or **it**.
> The robot cleaned **them**.

**Possessive** simply means that these particular pronouns are used to show *ownership*.

> That is **my** robot.
> That robot is **mine**.
> That is **our** robot.
> That robot is **ours**.
> That is **your** robot.
> That robot is **yours**.
> That is **his** or **her** or **its** robot.
> That robot is **his** or **hers** or **its**.
> That is **their** robot.
> That robot is **theirs**.

All clear? Good. Prove it by inserting the correct pronoun forms in the sentences below. Use the above examples as guides.

1. _____ (*3rd person masculine*) bought _____ (*3rd person feminine*) a brand-new kangaroo.

2. _____ all went to the store. (*1st person*)

3. Did _____ lose _____ new video cartridge? (*2nd person*)

4. Lena and Jim bought the robot; it is _____. (*3rd person*)

5. _____ (*1st person singular*) told Olga that after _____ (*1st person singular*) went to the laundromat, _____ (*1st person singular*) would call _____. (*3rd person singular*)

You will want to remember certain facts about pronouns.

**B. NOTES TO REMEMBER**

1. Never write: "Me and Jimmy went to the skating rink." It should be: "Jimmy and I went to the skating rink." You need the nominative case, *I*, not the objective case, *me*. As for putting the other person first, that's just courtesy.

2. The object of a preposition (just like the object of a verb) is in the objective case. Don't write—"We divided the candy between Jimmy and I." Do write—"We divided the candy between Jimmy and me."

3. Some pronouns sound like some contractions. Be wary of this type of mistake.

> **Your** is a possessive pronoun.
> **You're** is a contraction, meaning **you are.**
>
> **Its** is a possessive pronoun.
> **It's** is a contraction, meaning **it is.**
>
> **Their** is a possessive pronoun.
> **They're** is a contraction, meaning **they are.**

With these three notes in mind and your general knowledge of personal pronouns, substitute 16 correct pronouns for 16 incorrect ones in the paragraphs below. (Warning: some pronouns are already correct, so be careful as you set forth on this ''sweet'' assignment.) As a sample, the first pronoun has been corrected.

Maxie,
Morty,
and I
went on
a sweet
trip to
Mars.

The THREE MUSKETEERS, Maxie, Morty, and ~~me~~ [I], were taking the ROLO Rocket to MARS. (BABY RUTH was supposed to go along, but him was penalized for having BUTTERFINGER trouble when him dropped the ball on the MOUNDS in the ninth inning.) The rocket shot it's way along FIFTH AVENUE before takeoff so Maxie and Morty could wave to they're sponsor, MR. GOODBAR, and so he could wave to we adventurers.

As we blasted through space, two of we admired the SNO-CAPS below and the MILKY WAY above. But Maxie—her looked like a bent TWIZZLER. ''OH HENRY!'' she cried to Morty and I as the rocket began to jiggle and wiggle and she began to clutch her stomach. Soon all of we M & Ms (me name's Millie) felt like half-chewed TOOTSIE ROLLS, our misery made worse when us heard SNICKERS coming from our pilot, PETER PAUL.

Then his CHUCKLES stopped. ''The engines—their sputtering!'' shouted PETER PAUL.

''GO AHEAD!'' I ordered. ''We'll all end up as REESE'S PIECES anyway, the way your driving!''

Amazingly we arrived safely at MARS, and PETER PAUL divided the MARS bars (which serve only chocolate drinks) between Maxie, Morty, and I.

''It was a sweet trip,'' us M & Ms decided much later when we were back on earth. But perhaps not so sweet for PETER PAUL who had gone into *all* the MARS bars and was now a bit CHUNKY.

# 14

## PERSONAL PRONOUNS

## USE THEM!

When you write a story, even a brief one, your **point of view** determines which pronouns you will use.

*Point of view* is just that: the point from which a story is viewed. Suppose you wish to describe an automobile accident in which the young woman driver was seriously injured. You may describe it from the victim's point of view (1st person, the speaker, using "I") or from the author's point of view (3rd person, the person spoken about, using "she"). Which you decide to use depends on the end of the story *and* on your personal preference. Let's see how this works.

> I saw the shiny black Mercedes hurtling toward me, but it was too late to swerve, too late to stop, too late to do anything. Metal screeched against metal, and a swift, stabbing pain invaded my chest. I raised my hand to press the pain away, and my fingers were covered with warm wet blood. I was tired, incredibly tired, and my sight blurred, and I let my head droop wearily onto the broken steering wheel ...

That was the story told from a *1st person* point of view. Here's the same story told from a *3rd person* point of view.

> She saw the shiny black Mercedes hurtling toward her, but it was too late to swerve, too late to stop, too late to do anything. Metal screeched against metal, and a swift, stabbing pain invaded her chest. She raised her hand to press the pain away, and her fingers were covered with warm wet blood. She was tired, incredibly tired, and her sight blurred, and she let her head droop wearily onto the broken steering wheel. By the time the ambulance arrived, it was too late. She was dead.

As you can see, the two versions are almost identical—except for the last two sentences of the second version. If you plan to have your main character die at the end, you *must* use 3rd person. *No one* is clever enough to say: "By the time the ambulance arrived, it was too late. I was dead."

Below are several groups of sentences. In each case, two versions are given: one from the 3rd person point of view and one from the 1st. Decide which is better and explain your choice.

**1 a.** His wizened face shone in the darkness like a dried-up star-fish.

**b.** My wizened face shone in the darkness like a dried-up star-fish.

_____

_____

**2 a.** She seemed a levelheaded, friendly woman, her face strong and cheerful, her voice warm with confidence.

**b.** I seemed a levelheaded, friendly woman, my face strong and cheerful, my voice warm with confidence.

_____

_____

**3 a.** Her hair is beginning to turn. Her eyes grow dim. Her knees creak and her elbows sometimes refuse to work. She is, she fears, growing old.

**b.** My hair is beginning to turn. My eyes grow dim. My knees creak and my elbows sometimes refuse to work. I am, I fear, growing old.

_____

_____

**4 a.** He was taken to the emergency room, his eyes blank, his mouth wide open.

**b.** I was taken to the emergency room, my eyes blank, my mouth wide open.

_____

_____

**5 a.** During his lifetime he collected stamps, baseball cards, bone china, and letter openers. Before he tells you about his new collection, perhaps he should tell you what happened to all the old ones.

**b.** During my lifetime I have collected stamps, baseball cards, bone china, and letter openers. Before I tell you about my new collection, perhaps I should tell you what happened to all the old ones.

_____

_____

_____

70

Now answer these questions.

**6 a.** Is it easier to write a description of a character from a 1st or 3rd person point of view?_____ Why?_____

_____

_____

**b.** Is it easier to write one's own feelings and memories from a 1st or 3rd person point of view?_____ Why?_____

_____

_____

**B. WHICH POINT OF VIEW?**

This time we're dealing with *concepts*—ideas—rather than sentences. Which point of view (1st or 3rd) would probably be better to describe the following situations? Why?

**1.** A writer describes a mountaineering accident in which a young man falls and goes into a ten-day-long coma.

_____

_____

**2.** A sci-fi writer describes the same accident, but starts with the young man's fall and spends much time describing what is going on in the victim's mind *while* he is in a coma.

_____

_____

**3.** A writer describes a youth who is taking muscle-building exercises and is proud of his physique.

_____

_____

**4.** A writer writes a newspaper column about memories of his childhood.

_____

_____

**5.** A writer who lived through a San Francisco earthquake describes her experience.

_____

_____

Read the brief story printed below. It is written from the 1st person point of view.

> "Go ahead," I told myself. "Take it . . . before you turn chicken and run."
>
> I moved my hand stealthily toward the gold watch.
>
> Outside Kahn's Department Store, sleet had turned the city's skyscrapers to glittering ice palaces. I could pawn a watch like this, get enough for a room for a few days, maybe even for a week. I touched it. Warmth shot through me. I thought of a bed, four walls, quiet. Then I withdrew my hand abruptly. A few yards away, a man in a trench coat stood, his eyes dark and cold.
>
> "Pretty," I mumbled inadequately and walked away out into the storm.

Your job is to rewrite the story using the 3rd person point of view. On line 1, change the third word, "I," to a name (male or female). Then change all first person pronouns to third person pronouns. As you make the changes, copy the revised story below.

_____

_____

_____

_____

_____

_____

_____

_____

_____

_____

_____

_____

When you have finished, read both versions. Which do you prefer? There is no right or wrong answer. Whether you choose the first or the third person is usually a matter of preference—your preference.

Write sentences in accordance with the following instructions.

1.  Describe someone's face. Use the 3rd person point of view.

    _____

    _____

    _____

2.  Imagine yourself eating a piece of gooey pizza. _See_ yourself. Then describe the action, using a 1st person point of view.

    _____

    _____

    _____

3.  Describe a tree—any tree, using the 3rd person point of view.

    _____

    _____

    _____

4.  Describe the same tree, using the 1st person point of view. (Pretend you _are_ the tree.)

    _____

    _____

    _____

5.  Pinch one of your fingers—hard. Notice how the rest of your body reacts. What happens to your eyes? To your jaw? Describe this reaction, using a 1st person point of view.

    _____

    _____

    _____

6.  Describe a two year old eating a piece of pizza. Imagine yourself the two year old. Use a 1st person point of view.

    _____

    _____

    _____

7.  Describe your feeling the first time you tried something new (roller skating, skiing, washing the dishes, etc.). Use the 1st person point of view.

    _____

    _____

    _____

73

**8.** Describe an old man eating a piece of pizza. Imagine yourself the old man. Use a 1st person point of view.

_____

_____

_____

**9.** Describe an astronaut taking the first human steps on the planet Saturn. Use the 3rd person point of view.

_____

_____

_____

**10.** Describe the same astronaut taking the same first steps on the planet Saturn. Use the 1st person point of view.

_____

_____

_____

Are you beginning to see the possibilities that exist if you experiment with varying points of view? You should be!

# 15

## PERSONAL PRONOUNS

## USE THEM IN <u>YOUR</u> WRITING!

Three writing assignments: three chances to prove that you have mastered **point of view.**

**A.**  Fourteen-year-old Allie Jordan paused at the entrance of the new Youth Center and looked around. She saw . . .

____1____ to the right: a large, brand-new ping-pong table

_____ to the left: a large basketball court

_____ straight ahead, at the back: several arcade games

_____ to the far right, beyond the ping-pong table: a dozen card tables, with chairs, all painted bright red or green

_____ to the near left, close to the doorway: a small lounge area with comfortable chairs and shelves filled with books and magazines.

First organize the above notes *spatially*. What does Allie first see when she looks to the right? Label that item #1. Then move in a *counter-clockwise* ↰ movement, from right to left, assigning suitable numbers to the other notes.

Finished? You now have an outline, organized *spatially* (according to where things are located in space).

Write a description of the Youth Center *from Allie's point of view* (3rd person point of view). We've provided the first sentence and a half. You continue.

Fourteen-year-old Allie paused at the entrance of the new Youth Center. She gasped with delight when she saw the gleaming new ping-pong table to the right, and her eyes opened even wider when she noticed . . . . .

_____

_____

_____

_____

_____

_____

_____

_____

_____

_____

_____

_____

_____

_____

_____

_____

_____

**B.** This time *you* are walking into an old, deserted haunted house. You walk through the half-broken door and look around you.

**1.** What brushes against your forehead almost immediately?

_____

_____

**2.** Look up. What do you see above you?

_____

_____

**3.** Step forward. Look down. What do you see (and hear)?

_____

_____

**4.** What do you see to your left? (It may be a piece of furniture, an unusual wall, or a painting ... or something else.)

_____

_____

**5.** What do you see straight ahead?

_____

_____

**6.** What do you see to your right?

_____

_____

You now have an outline, organized spatially, of a room in a haunted house. Notice that this time we moved from the left to the right, in a *clockwise* ⌒↘ movement. When you organize spatially, you may move in any direction as long as the direction is consistent.

Use your outline as a guide as you write a descriptive paragraph of this room. Remember: as you write, you are using a first person point of view—*yours*. We have provided the first sentence.

Fists clenched and heart pounding, I forced myself through the half-broken door of the haunted house.

_____

_____

_____

_____

_____

_____

_____

_____

_____

_____

_____

_____

_____

_____

_____

_____

_____

_____

Check your writing. This type of description *demands* shivery verbs and nouns, cobwebbed adjectives and adverbs. Did you use them?

**C.** This time describe a small shop (grocery store, pizza parlor, any type) in your neighborhood. Decide: will you describe this shop from right to left, or from left to right? _____

Next, make notes below—organized *spatially*. (Include as many details as possible. Not just—cans of soup; but—cans of tomato soup, and bean soup, and oyster stew. Not just—a cash register; but—a battered, dusty-brown cash register with three keys missing and a splintered money drawer.)

_____

_____

_____

_____

_____

_____

_____

_____

_____

_____

_____

_____

_____

_____

_____

_____

Decide: will you write the description from a first person point of view ("I") or from a third person point of view ("he" or "she")?

_____

You are ready. Write your description as vividly as you can. Try to include some colors and smells to sharpen your picture.

_____

_____

_____

_____

_____

_____

_____

_____

_____

_____

_____

_____

_____

_____

_____

_____

_____

_____

_____

_____

_____

WRITING TECHNIQUE

# 5

One of the first problems every writer encounters is— "Shall I tell this story from the 1st or 3rd person point of view?" The answer depends on the story itself and on the writer—on *you*!

STEP VI

# ARE

# YOU

# WITH

# IT?

# USE

# PURPOSEFUL

# PREPOSITIONS

THE SIXTH STEP TO BETTER WRITING is to use **_purposeful_**
**_prepositions._** Prepositions will help you to write clearly and
concisely.

> *Why say . . .?*
>
> A Little Leaguer has parents. Parents
> think a baseball game is simply a
> nervous breakdown. A baseball game
> has innings.
>
> *Why not say* (as Earl Wilson did) . . .?
>
> "**For** the parents **of** a Little Leaguer, a
> baseball game is simply a nervous
> breakdown divided **into** innings."

Much better? Of course—thanks to the small seemingly
unimportant **preposition!**

**"Parents think a baseball game is simply a nervous
breakdown . . ."**

# 16

## PURPOSEFUL PREPOSITIONS
## LEARN THEM!

Your mother cries frantically: "Where is your little sister?" And you calmly reply:

> She's (**under** the racing car).
> She's (**in** the monkey's cage).
> She's (**with** the Abominable Snowman).
> She's (**on** the highest trapeze).
> She's (**at** the edge **of** the cliff).
> She's (**near** the dragon).

Any one of your six replies would tell your mother *where* your little sister is (though none would allay her fears). In each reply, the boldfaced word is the preposition, and the words within the parentheses form the prepositional phrase. At the end of the phrase is a noun.

This may help to dramatize your little sister's whereabouts. Imagine the six explanations as the blades of a fan, all radiating from *she's*. Like this . . .

### A. PLAYING WITH PREPOSITIONS

She's

**under** the racing car.
**in** the monkey's cage.
**with** the Abominable Snowman.
**on** the highest trapeze.
**at** the edge **of** the cliff.
**near** the dragon.

1. Create your own fan by dreaming up *six* replies, each using a different prepositional phrase, for the following question:

Where is your basketball?

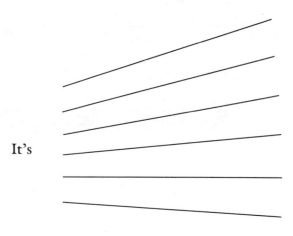

It's

2. Create another fan by developing *five* prepositional phrases, any one of which would complete the following sentence satisfactorily:

The duck waddled . . . . . . .

The duck waddled

3. Create one more fan (but an imaginary one this time) by developing *five* prepositional phrases, any one of which would complete the following sentence satisfactorily:

The escaped convict hid . . . . . . .

Prepositional phrases tell something about a verb or a noun.

**a.** Phrases that tell something about *verbs* act as **adverbs.**

> I jogged *around the lake.*
>
> I jogged *until noon.*
>
> I jogged *despite the light rain.*

Adverbial prepositional phrases are diagrammed like this:

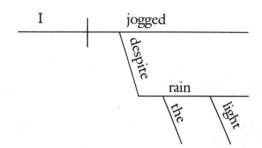

> A *diagram* is a drawing that usually shows the relationship among the parts of a sentence.

**b.** Phrases that describe *nouns* act as **adjectives.**

> The woman *behind the counter* teaches English.
>
> The woman *in the red dress* teaches English.
>
> The woman *with a bandaged hand* teaches English.

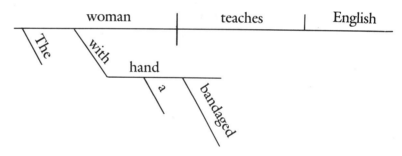

Now it's *your* turn. In each of the following sentences, underline the prepositional phrase, state whether it is used as an adverb or adjective, and diagram it.

ADJ. *or* ADV.

**1.** The girl with red hair is called "Rusty."          1 _____

**85**

**2.** The typist slipped into her coat.        2 _____

What coat is put on wet
and never has buttons?

A coat of paint.

**3.** Eighteen newborn opossums fit in one tea-
spoon.        3 _____

**4.** The first soda pop was concocted in 1807.        4 _____

**5.** The barbers of ancient Rome also extracted
teeth.        5 _____

Where does a sheep get
its hair cut?

At the baa-baa shop, of
course!

Finally—use your imagination and skill to create a good prepositional phrase that will complete each of the following sentences. To help you get started, we have suggested prepositions for the first three sentences.

1. The most popular game (**in** _____)
   is Monopoly.

2. The baker couldn't find any flour (**in** _____)
   so he made the bread (**with** _____).

3. (**At** _____), the children filled their
   pails (**with** _____).

4. (_____), the astronaut
   walked (_____).

5. (_____), the children skated.

6. The champion boxer (_____)
   knocked out the challenger (_____).

7. He stared (_____) and shivered un-
   controllably.

8. The front-wheel tire rolled (_____),
   and the flashy Jaguar plunged (_____).

9. The explorer climbed (_____) carrying a radio (_____).

10. The elephant (_____) trampled
    (_____) (_____).

# 17

# PURPOSEFUL PREPOSITIONS
## USE THEM!

You can cram your sentences with information if you use **prepositional phrases** effectively. Here's how to do it.

First practice—by combining sentences. Notice that the prepositional phrase may be placed at the beginning, or at the end, or in the middle of the new sentence.

A. COMBINING SENTENCES

### AT THE BEGINNING:

**It was a cold day. It was raining. Justin set out to find his lost fox terrier.**

> Change sentence 1 to <u>On a cold day</u>
> 2 to <u>in the rain</u>
>
> Place both prepositional phrases, in that order, at the beginning of sentence 3. Both phrases tell us *when* "Justin set out."

**On a cold day, in the rain, Justin set out to find his lost fox terrier.**

### AT THE END:

**The hang-gliding tournament was won by a young woman. The young woman had black, curly hair.**

> Change sentence 2 to <u>with black, curly hair</u> and place the phrase after *woman*. The phrase tells us *what kind of* woman.

**The hang-gliding tournament was won by a young woman with black, curly hair.**

### IN THE MIDDLE:

**That book costs $12.98. Its cover is dark green.**

> Change sentence 2 to <u>with the dark green cover.</u>. This time put the prepositional phrase after *book*. Now the phrase tells us *what kind of* book.

**That book <u>with the dark green cover</u> costs $12.98.**

| SOME COMMON PREPOSITIONS | |
| --- | --- |
| after | in |
| along | into |
| among | near |
| around | of |
| at | on |
| behind | through |
| despite | to |
| during | under |
| for | until |
| from | with |

It's your turn now. Combine the sentences in each cluster below into one good sentence, using one or more prepositional phrases.

1. The doctor told the patient the bad news. His voice was low and gruff.

   _____

   _____

2. Michelle headed for the ocean and a joyful hour of riding the waves. She carried her surfboard under her arm.

   _____

   _____

3. Jim went to the hockey game. His little sister, Kerry, went with him.

   _____

   _____

4. It was midnight. Three gnomes perched on the highest hill. They were wearing small green suits. (Change sentences 1 and 3 to prepositional phrases.)

   _____

   _____

5. Jessica went shopping. She wanted an umbrella. She wanted a raincoat. (Change sentences 2 and 3 to prepositional phrases.)

   _____

   _____

6. It was Saturday. Ten boys went camping. Their destination was the Adirondack woods. (Change sentences 1 and 3 to prepositional phrases.)

   _____

   _____

7. A lost little boy found himself in a dark forest. Only his dog kept him company.

   _____

   _____

**89**

8. Jake traveled fifty miles in one day. He rode a skateboard.

   _____

9. Mrs. Kee called the dentist. She wanted an appointment.

   _____

10. Carlos raked leaves. He earned $4 an hour.

    _____

Continue practice—by creating sentences.

## B. CREATING SENTENCES

EXAMPLE:    **Two boys swam** _____ .

   Where?        *in the Atlantic Ocean*
   How long?     *for six hours*
   Why?          *for a $20,000 prize*

REVISION:   Two boys swam for six hours in the Atlantic Ocean for a $20,000 prize.

   OR:   For six hours two boys swam in the Atlantic Ocean for a $20,000 prize.

   OK? Just answer each question with a prepositional phrase; then add the prepositional phrases to the original sentence and you will have created a new, information-packed sentence. Remember: prepositional phrases may be inserted at the beginning, in the middle, or at the end.

1.  **A gang war broke out . . .**

    Where? _____

    When? _____

    Who was involved? _____

    New sentence: _____

    _____

    _____

2.  **He asked her to go diving . . .**

    Why? _____

    Where? _____

    When? _____

    New sentence: _____

    _____

    _____

**90**

**3.** **Elizabeth and Michael climbed . . .**

Where? _____

How long? _____

When? _____

What kind of day was it? _____

New sentence: _____

_____

_____


**4.** **John wore new jeans . . .**

What color? _____

What kind of label? _____

Where was the label? _____

New sentence: _____

_____

_____


**5.** **Althea bought a small white elephant . . .**

Made of what? _____

How much did she spend? _____

What kind of tusks did it have? _____

New sentence: _____

_____

_____

> **Why is an elephant such a good traveler?**
>
> **Because it always has its trunk with it.**

A reporter just handed in the following story. Read it.

C. PLAY A PROOFREADER

> [1]A Banana Olympics was held at Beloit College in Wisconsin. [2]The year was 1984. [3]Ten teams competed. [4]There was a banana eating match. [5]There was a banana hunt. [6]There was a Banana Punt, Pass, and Kick competition. [7]One "fun" event was the Diving for Bananas Contest. [8]The contest was held in a swimming pool. [9]Bananas were on the bottom. [10]The winner recovered 76 bananas in thirty seconds.

You realize at once that the paragraph will be much more interesting if the short choppy sentences are combined. Do so—using prepositonal phrases. (A few hints are given.) Write your revision below.

1. Combine sentences 1 and 2. This is so easy you don't need a hint.

2. Combine sentences 3, 4, 5, and 6. Turn 4, 5, and 6 into prepositional phrases; then add them to sentence 3.

3. Combine sentences 8, 9, and 10. This is tricky. Make 10 the first part of the sentence. Turn 8 and 9 into prepositional phrases and add to 10.

_____

_____

_____

_____

_____

_____

_____

_____

_____

_____

_____

Read both the original item and your revision. Which is better?

92

# 18

## PURPOSEFUL PREPOSITIONS

## USE THEM IN <u>YOUR</u> WRITING!

████████████████████████████████

*Input* is the term used to describe information fed into a computer. Below are several questions followed by "input." Your task is to use the input—the information—to answer the questions clearly and concisely. (Prepositional phrases will be useful.)

**A.** What is Big Rock Candy Mountain? (Use two sentences.)

      *Input:* an imaginary land
            location: the U.S.
            hoboes and tramps live there
            dogs have rubber teeth
            jails are made of tin

    *Your answer:* Big Rock Candy Mountain is _____

_____

_____

_____

_____

_____

**B.** Describe an unusual two-car collision. (Use one sentence.)

      *Input:* location: Ohio
            time: 1895
            only two cars existed in the whole state
            they collided

    *Your answer:* An unusual two-car collision occurred _____

_____

_____

_____

**C.** What is Cockaigne (also spelled Cockayne)? (Use two sentences.)

Input: an imaginary land
location: possibly France
people who love to eat live there
houses of hard sugar; streets paved with pastry
stores require no money from customers

Your answer: Cockaigne is _____

_____

_____

_____

_____

_____

_____

_____

**D.** Describe an unusual wedding. (Use three sentences.)

Input: location: Chicago
time: 1984
ceremony held: in large cage
inside cage: bride and groom; clergyman; best man and matron of honor; four Bengal tigers; three African lions
quotation: the bride said: "I'm a little nervous."

Your answer: An unusual wedding took place _____

_____

_____

_____

_____

_____

_____

_____

_____

**E.** Describe an unusual burglary. (Use three or four sentences.)

*Input:* location: Schurra's Candy Factory, San Jose, California

time: just before Easter

method: someone broke front window of store

theft: someone stole 40-pound, 3-foot-high chocolate bunny—nothing else

reward: owner offered jelly beans—five pounds

police investigation: no suspects; thief may have eaten the evidence

*Your answer:* A thief with a sweet tooth _____

_____

_____

_____

_____

_____

_____

_____

_____

_____

Before you continue, reread your five answers and underline every prepositional phrase. How many prepositional phrases did you use? _____ Convinced now that prepositional phrases are useful?

*WRITING TECHNIQUE*

# 6 ▬▬▬▬▬▬▬▬▬▬▬

**Use the prepositional phrase to write sentences (and paragraphs) packed with information. This technique is as handy (and necessary) as a suitcase on a long trip!**

# WRITING TIME—II

By now, you have acquired some skill in working with nouns and adjectives, verbs and adverbs, pronouns and prepositions. You are ready for some practice in "fleshing out" bare skeletons . . . to use words and details to make a character or an incident come alive.

Let's start with this paragraph.

It was a cold January day. Kris walked into the restaurant and put a dollar bill on the counter. "Coffee and a doughnut," he said.

The paragraph is barely adequate. It tells us what Kris did; it tells us a little about the weather. But it doesn't tell us what kind of man Kris is, or what his mood is.

We ask ourselves some questions:

- What was Kris wearing? (a thin overcoat)
- How cold was it? (piercing)
- How did he walk into the restaurant? (he stumbled)
- What kind of restaurant was it? (all-night diner)
- How did he put the dollar bill on the counter? (dropped it wearily)
- What tone of voice did he use when he ordered? (whining)

The result will be something like this:

With only a thin overcoat to shield him from the piercing January cold, Kris stumbled into the all-night diner. Wearily he dropped a dirty dollar bill on the counter. "Coffee and a doughnut," he whined.

Now we have many more clues. We can guess that Kris is broke, that the dollar bill may be his last one, and that he's about ready to give up. We can almost *see* Kris.

If we had answered the questions differently, we might instead have come up with this . . .

Kris dashed into the fast-food restaurant and slapped a dollar bill on the counter. After a quick glance at his watch, he snapped: "Coffee and a doughnut—and make it fast!"

This is a totally different Kris—a Kris in a hurry—a Kris with something important to do—a Kris who's aggressive and confident. *Details* make the difference!

"Flesh out" each of the following bare skeletons. Remember: add details that will give your reader a sharp vivid picture of the incident.

1. **As the piece of cake went over her head, she ducked. "Don't do that again," she said to the boy.**

   **a.** What kind of cake? What size was the piece?_____
   _____

   **b.** What is a more dramatic verb to replace "went"? _____
   _____

   **c.** *How* did "she" duck? Add an adverb. _____

   **d.** Who is the boy—her son, her brother, her nephew?
   _____ How old is he? _____

   **e.** What is a more exact verb to replace "say"? _____

   *Your revision:*

   _____
   _____
   _____
   _____
   _____

2. **Lisa held out her hand. "Please give me some money," she said.**

   **a.** How old is Lisa? _____

   **b.** How much money is she asking for? _____

   **c.** Why does she want money? _____
   _____

   **d.** What is a more exact, stronger verb to replace "said"? __
   _____

   *Your revision:*

   _____
   _____
   _____
   _____
   _____

97

Below is a rather dull paragraph about an exciting incident. Read it.

> After school, I started to walk home. I wanted some pizza. I thought I'd stop at the pizza place and get a couple of slices. While I was walking along the street, I saw a big expensive car go through the red light and hit a small old car. There was a big noise. The driver of the big car got out and started to yell at the driver of the small car. I didn't like that. I went over and told the driver of the big car that I'd seen the whole thing. A police officer came along and I told her everything I'd seen. The driver of the big car didn't like that. But I had seen it all. By the time everything was settled, it was too late for pizza.

Your job? To revise it.

*First:* Make any changes you like in sentence structure. Combine sentences, using prepositional phrases. Rearrange them.

*Second:* Cross out weak verbs and replace them with exact, action-packed ones.

*Third:* Cross out general nouns and replace with specific ones.

*Fourth:* Add any adjectives that will make the picture sharper and clearer.

*Fifth:* Add any adverbs that will contribute to the action.

*Sixth:* When you are satisfied, copy your revision below.

**WORDS TO DESCRIBE AN INCIDENT**

collide
smash
amble
sedan
witness
scream
stroll
yearn
speed
munch
screeching
convertible
desperately
huge
shatter

_____
_____
_____
_____
_____
_____
_____
_____
_____
_____
_____
_____
_____
_____
_____

Reread the original paragraph and your revision. Isn't *your* version considerably better? Sharper? More interesting? What you did with someone else's paragraph, you can do with your own. Try it below.

First read the following information. (*It's true!*)

C. YOU'RE ON YOUR OWN!

SETTING:       a bank in Barcelona, Spain, Sept. 5, 1982.
CHARACTER:   a thief known as The Fat Sparrow.
ACTION:        thief entered bank carrying cage of parakeets. He released the parakeets. Customers and cashiers climbed on tables and counters trying to catch the birds. Thief used long-handled pincers to reach through teller's window. Thief picked up bundles of banknotes and disappeared. He left the parakeets behind.

Pretend you are a reporter. The above information came over the teletype, and you have been told to write it up as a feature filler: a short, interesting story that will capture readers' attention and amuse them. Write it. (Consider using a *chronological* organization of the material. See page 60.)

**ACTION VERBS**

snatch
dart
scramble
scatter
zoom
hover
scale
abandon
soar
flutter
swarm
capture
flit
glide
leap

Now read your own paragraph. Is it as good as it can be? Is it lively? Amusing? Have you used strong action verbs and specific nouns? Have you used a few "different" and startling adjectives? Have you used prepositional phrases to eliminate short sentences? Revise. Replace. Add. Then copy your revised paragraph below.

_____

_____

_____

_____

_____

_____

_____

_____

_____

_____

_____

_____

_____

_____

If you worked hard at building each sentence, you should be feeling rather proud of the result!

WHERE?

THERE.

GO.

OH!

USE

ALL

FOUR

TYPES OF

SENTENCES

THE SEVENTH STEP TO BETTER WRITING is to use all four types of sentences: the **_declarative_**, the **_interrogative_**, the **_imperative_**, and the **_exclamatory_**.

> **Declarative:** "I don't care what is written about me—so long as it isn't true." (*Katharine Hepburn*)
>
> **Interrogative:** "What's up, Doc?" (*Bugs Bunny*)
>
> **Imperative:** "Be nice to people on your way up because you meet 'em on your way down." (*Jimmy Durante*)
>
> **Exclamatory:** "They'll have to bury me before I retire, and even then my tombstone will read: 'I'll be back!'" (*Vincent Price*)

Using one type of sentence only is like using one tone of voice—you soon bore even yourself! To avoid boring yourself and your readers, **use all four types of sentences.**

# 19
## FOUR TYPES OF SENTENCES
## LEARN THEM!

"Variety is the spice of life," says an old proverb. Well, spice both your writing and your speaking by using all *four* types of sentences:

> DECLARATIVE
> INTERROGATIVE
> IMPERATIVE
> EXCLAMATORY

### A. THE DECLARATIVE

The **declarative** sentence is simply a statement. You probably use this most of the time.

> I took a stroll.

> I took a stroll along the Milky Way and met three Martians, two Venusians, and the captain of a long-lost space rocket from the U.S.S.R.

Both are declarative sentences. Declarative sentences may be long or short, simple or complicated—but always they simply make a statement. (Remember to use a period after each declarative sentence.)

**1.** Write a *short* declarative sentence.

_____

**2.** Write a *long* declarative sentence.

_____

_____

### B. THE INTERROGATIVE

The **interrogative** sentence is a question.

> Do you like sour pickles?
> Would you like to go to the movies?
> Have you bought a birthday present for your little brother?

**1.** Write an interrogative sentence.

_____

**2.** There is a special kind of interrogative sentence that is useful in writing: the **rhetorical** question. This is a question that you do *not* want anyone else to answer. You are asking it so that *you* can answer it. (Remember to use a question mark [?] after each interrogative sentence.)

EXAMPLE:

A public speaker declares that the middle-class is the backbone of the American system. (*Then he asks a rhetorical question.*) "Are we going to let the middle-class be taxed out of existence?" (*Next he answers his own question.*) "No, we are not! And here's what we can do about it!"

ANOTHER EXAMPLE:

Your brother and some of his pals broke the family video game. Your parents have had it repaired, but they announce that neither you nor your brother will be permitted to use it for six weeks. You try to change their minds by using a series of rhetorical questions—and answers.

"Did *I* break the game? No, I didn't."
"Was *I* careless? No, I wasn't,"
"Should *I* suffer for something I didn't do? No, that's not acceptable in any civilized country in the world!"
"So—why can't *I* use the video game?"

The last question, of course, is a real question: one you want your parents to answer. But the three questions that preceded it gave you a chance to give the answers and to make some powerful points.

**a.** Here is an advertisement for new cars. Notice that the first sentence is missing. Read the "ad." Then write a rhetorical question that can act as the opening sentence.

---

You should buy a new car now because...
- cars will be more expensive next year,
- this year's model uses rubber tires, while next year's will use plastic tires, and
- (most important of all) no cars will be manufactured next year, according to the Department of Defense.

**b.** Here's another incomplete ad. Again, supply the missing first sentence: a rhetorical question.

---

Sizzling Soda is good for you! It builds muscles, sweetens your breath, and increases your intelligence. Buy Sizzling Soda today and have a sizzling tomorrow!

**c.** A senator introduces a bill that would force all students to attend school for the full twelve months of the year. You disagree vehemently and decide to write a Letter to the Editor. Develop a rhetorical question that would serve as a good beginning for your letter.

_____

_____

_____

**d.** You have been asked to write an essay for your social studies class. You decide a *series* of rhetorical questions would provide a good introductory paragraph.

EXAMPLE: (for an essay about reluctant American voters)

Why do so few American voters find the energy to pull the lever on election day? Why do John and Jane Doe sit at home watching TV rather than make a choice that will affect their own futures? Why are so many of us reluctant to vote—when Thomas Jefferson and Patrick Henry and George Washington, only 200 years ago, were ready to fight and die for the very same right?

YOUR TURN NOW:
(for an essay about _____ )

_____

_____

_____

_____

_____

_____

_____

_____

_____

_____

_____

_____

_____

The **imperative** sentence gives a command.

> Go to the store *now*.
> Wash your hands.
> Do your homework.
> Clean your room.

## C. THE IMPERATIVE

(Your parents are probably experts and can deliver imperative sentences without much thought.) *You* apply some thought and develop imperative sentences that would be appropriate in the following situations:

1.  Your little sister just snitched your diary.

    _____

2.  Your dog (yours, not your family's) just broke your mother's favorite lamp, your father's new spotlight for the car, and your own new expensive portable radio.

    _____

3.  You are trying to teach some seven year olds how to roll up a sleeping bag. They're talking and laughing and paying no attention to you.

    _____

## D. THE EXCLAMATORY

The **exclamatory** sentence simply exclaims—or shows astonishment.

> I can't believe it!
> Oh, no! Not again!
> "You asked for it!"
> No! Never!

(Your parents are probably experts at delivering exclamatory sentences, too!) Become an expert yourself and develop exclamatory sentences appropriate in the following situations. (Remember to use an exclamation mark [!] after each exclamatory sentence.)

1.  You went in swimming alone. Suddenly you are caught in an undertow. You go down once. Then you come to the surface again. Your exclamation?

    _____

**2.** Your sister knows you can't refuse a dare. She dares you to take the first dive from the springboard. Your exclamation?

_____

**3.** Your best friend borrowed your $350 stereo equipment and left it on a bench in the shopping mall. When she went back for it, it was gone. She tells you that it may still show up. Your exclamation?

_____

**E. PROBLEM TIME**

Duke, your dog, has just broken your mother's favorite vase. You are furious with him, and when your mother walks in, she is furious with both of you.

Following the formula below, write the dialogue that might take place.

MOTHER: (use an _imperative_ sentence) _____

_____

YOU: (use a _declarative_ sentence followed by an _interrogative_ sentence) _____

_____

MOTHER: (use an _exclamatory_ sentence) _____

_____

The trick, of course, is to know _when_ to use each type of sentence. More about this later. At least now you know that there _are_ four types of sentences that you can use as needed.

> **DECLARATIVE: A statement makes—**
> "We baked a pie." "We iced some cakes."
>
> **INTERROGATIVE: A question poses—**
> "Shall I go?" "Who snitched my roses?"
>
> **IMPERATIVE: A command decrees—**
> "Do your homework." "Eat your peas."
>
> **EXCLAMATORY: Strong feeling shows—**
> "Fire!" or "Help!" or "How he grows!"

# 20

## FOUR TYPES OF SENTENCES
## USE THEM!

The more often you use all four types of sentences, the better servants they will become. Soon they will be "on call" whenever you need them.

**A. TRANSFORMING SENTENCES**

With a little thought, a declarative sentence can be turned into an interrogative, or an imperative into a declarative. Like this . . .

*Declarative:*    The hailstones are larger than golf balls.

*Interrogative:*  Are the hailstones larger than golf balls?

And this . . .

*Imperative:*  Go to the skating rink this afternoon.

*Declarative:*  I wish you would go to the skating rink this afternoon.

YOUR TURN . . .

1. *Declarative:*    The ugliest animal in the zoo is the warthog.

   *Interrogative:*  _____

   _____

2. *Interrogative:*  Is the South Pole covered with 8,850 feet of solid ice?

   *Declarative:*  _____

   _____

3. *Declarative:*  It seems that I won a million dollars in the lottery.

   *Exclamatory:*  _____

   _____

4. *Imperative:*  Clean your room.

   *Interrogative:*  _____

—— • ——

The *versatile* writer
can turn from one
sentence type to
another.

—— • ——

**5.** *Imperative:*    List all your talents below.

    *Declarative:*    _____

**6.** *Declarative:*    We would appreciate it if you would send a check immediately.

    *Imperative:*    _____

**7.** *Exclamatory:*    You can't mean it!

    *Declarative:*    _____

**8.** *Interrogative:*    Why do you always do your homework at 5 a.m.?

    *Exclamatory:*    _____

                 _____

## B. WRITING TO ORDER

Another way to train yourself to use all four types of sentences is to write a few paragraphs—to order. Below, you are given an assignment and a list of the types of sentences to use as you fulfill the assignment.

**1.** Start with a quotation by a celebrity.

> *"My whole life I've been trying to prove I'm not just yesterday."* (Jackie Cooper)

[1]Jackie Cooper once said, "My whole life I've been trying to prove I'm not just yesterday." [2]What did the well-known actor mean? [3]For those who remember Jackie the child star, his meaning is obvious. [4]Fans see in the mature Cooper the child that he was . . . not the adult that he is. [5]Poor Jackie!

*Formula:*
[1]Quotation—notice use of quotation marks.
[2]Rhetorical question.
[3]Declarative sentence.
[4]Declarative sentence.
[5]Exclamatory sentence.

YOUR QUOTATION: *"No one knows what to say in the loser's room."* (Muhammad Ali, the boxing champ)

Write a paragraph discussing the meaning of Muhammad Ali's quotation. Follow the formula to the right of the Cooper paragraph.

_____

_____

_____

_____

_____

_____

2.  You have just been accused of stealing 5¢ from the Candy Sale. Your assignment: Defend yourself against the accusation. Do this in a brief, four-sentence paragraph.

    FORMULA:  First sentence: I have been accused of stealing 5¢ from the Candy Sale.

    Second sentence: a rhetorical question.

    Third sentence: an exclamatory sentence answering the rhetorical question.

    Fourth sentence: a declarative sentence commenting on the accusation.

    YOUR PARAGRAPH:

    _____

    _____

    _____

    _____

    _____

    _____

3.  Your older sister or brother or friend gives you an order that you think is unfair. Give the order and your reaction in a four-sentence paragraph.

    FORMULA:  First sentence: an imperative sentence repeating the order, in quotes. (For example: "Walk twenty miles before dinner," my sister ordered.)

    Second sentence: a declarative sentence commenting on the order.

    Third sentence: an interrogative sentence—a rhetorical question.

    Fourth sentence: an exclamatory sentence that closes the argument.

    YOUR PARAGRAPH:

    _____

    _____

    _____

    _____

    _____

    _____

As your final step in learning to use all four types of sentences in your writing, we are going to barrage you with six quick assignments. Each requires an answer of only *two* sentences, but—the two sentences must be of different types. Try various combinations of types until you hit upon the one that is just right.

## C. A BARRAGE OF SHORT PARAGRAPHS

EXAMPLE: *What is your favorite food?*

Who wouldn't love spaghetti, drowning in sauce and smothered in cheese? It's small wonder that spaghetti is my favorite food.

(interrogative + declarative sentences)

Ready? Go!

**1.** *Who is your favorite entertainer?*

_____

_____

_____

_____

(The two types of sentences used: _____)

**2.** *What do you like to do in your spare time?*

_____

_____

_____

_____

(The two types of sentences used: _____)

**3.** *If you could go anywhere in the world, what country or city would you choose to visit?*

_____

_____

_____

_____

(The two types of sentences used: _____)

111

**4.** *What food do you dislike so much you think it should be outlawed?*

_____

_____

_____

_____

(The two types of sentences used: _____)

**5.** *What fictitious character do you most admire? (It may be from a novel, from TV, from a movie.)*

_____

_____

_____

_____

(The two types of sentences used: _____)

**6.** *Describe your position in your family. Are you the oldest, the youngest, or in the middle? Are you an only child, or one of a large group?*

_____

_____

_____

_____

(The two types of sentences used: _____)

# 21

## FOUR TYPES OF SENTENCES
## USE THEM IN **YOUR** WRITING!

Put all four types of sentences to work in the assignments that follow. How? We'll show you. It's easy! (See? We just did it!)

**A.** Learn a little about yourself by completing the three lists below. (Be honest!)

**MAKE A STATEMENT.**
**(End with a period.)**

**ASK A QUESTION.**
**(End with a question mark.)**

**GIVE A COMMAND.**
**(End with a period.)**

**EXPRESS STRONG FEELING.**
**(End with an exclamation point.)**

1.  List three things you like. (Think of specific foods, weather, activities, anything.)

    _____

    _____

    _____

2.  List three things you dislike.

    _____

    _____

    _____

3.  List three things you fear.

    _____

    _____

    _____

You now have the material to write a paragraph organized *categorically*.

A **category** is a group of related things. For example, THINGS YOU LIKE would form one category; THINGS YOU DISLIKE would form a second category; and THINGS YOU FEAR would form a third.

Read the paragraph below. Notice its pattern: it begins with a question, continues with three declarative sentences, and ends with an exclamation. Write a paragraph, following the same pattern but using your own notes.

> What kind of person am I? I like raw onions, long bouts of Monopoly, and swimming in the rain. I dislike nightmares (especially about fires), mushy vegetables, and unleashed dogs. I am afraid of tornadoes, chipmunks, and—of course—nuclear war. If that makes me a peace-loving, onion-crunching Monopoly player, so be it!

**THE PATTERN:**
- **an interrogative sentence**
- **three declarative sentences**
- **an exclamatory sentence**

_____
_____
_____
_____
_____
_____
_____
_____
_____
_____
_____

**B.** This time use the same sort of organization (categorical), but with different material: *Animals as Pets*.

Read the paragraph on the next page and notice that it follows this pattern:

1. imperative sentence (used within a quotation)

2. rhetorical question

3. three declarative sentences, each dealing with a different category: dogs, horses, snakes

4. rhetorical question

5. concluding exclamation

> "Buy your child a pet," say the psychologists. But what kind of pet? Dogs are loyal, but they're also noisy and not very useful. Horses are useful—they can pull a plow if you live on a farm—but they're a bit big for a child to cuddle in bed. Snakes are useful, too: they eat rodents; and they're small enough (some of them) to cuddle. But who wants a snake around the house? One obvious solution—buy your child a pet rock!

*Your turn*. Write your own paragraph—organized categorically—about animals (three kinds) as pets. Follow the pattern outlined above.

_____

_____

_____

_____

_____

_____

_____

_____

_____

_____

_____

**C.** **Snacks!** What could be more important? The U.S. has become a nation of snackers, snacking hungrily from waking to sleeping. Some people even spend restless nights, thanks to the cake crumbs and broken potato chips that accompany them to bed. Start your investigation by describing three *categories* of snacks. For one category we chose crackers.

EXAMPLE—*Crackers*: Crackers make fine snacks because they come in so many varieties. One can indulge in saltines with cream cheese, grahams with peanut butter, or wheat chips with cheddar.

Your three categories:

**1.** _____

_____

**HAVE SOME SNACKS.**   _____

115

**2.** _____

_____

_____

**3.** _____

_____

_____

Fine. You now have enough material for a good essay about snacks. Your angle . . .

*Snacking is a marvelous habit.*

OR    *Snacking is an atrocious habit.*

PROCEDURE:

**1.** Which angle do you choose?_____

**2.** On scrap paper, develop your angle in an introductory paragraph. For example: *why* is snacking marvelous (or atrocious)?

**3.** Still working on scrap paper, develop one category of snacks into a paragraph. Use plenty of details.

**4.** Develop a second category of snacks into a paragraph.

**5.** Develop a third category of snacks into a paragraph.

**6.** Now (still on scrap paper) write a concluding paragraph. Two possible approaches: good effects of snacking; bad effects of snacking. You may wish to be a bit humorous or sarcastic in the conclusion.

**7.** You now have, on scrap paper, a complete essay: introduction, three developing paragraphs, and a conclusion. Check it against the following checklist.

Did you use at least *three* types of sentences?

Did you use specific nouns and action verbs?

Did you use a few really good adjectives and adverbs?

Do any revision that is appropriate.

**CLEVER TITLE**

**Try...**

**Rhyme or
Alliteration or
A Rhetorical Question.**

**Try...**

**A Startling Fact or
A Pun or
A Quotation.**

**8.** Provide a clever title for your essay; write *it* and your essay below.

_____

_____

_____

_____

_____

_____

[*continued*]

# 7

Since there are four types of sentences, *use* all four. Don't settle for one dull declarative sentence after another. That's like trying to run a car on one cylinder when four are available!

IT'S

REALLY

NOT

SIMPLE

AT

ALL!

USE

COMPOUND

SENTENCES

THE EIGHTH STEP TO BETTER WRITING is to use **compound** sentences: sentences created by combining two or more simple sentences. Think of a compound sentence as a bargain: two for the price of one!

> *"It's very hard to climb the ladder,* (and) *it's very easy to go down the slide."*
> (Debbie Reynolds)
>
> *"They've great respect for the dead in Hollywood,* (but) *none for the living."*
> (Errol Flynn)
>
> *"Pick your enemies carefully,* (or) *you'll never make it in Los Angeles."*
> (Rona Barrett)

Compound sentences eliminate too many short, choppy sentences and contribute a new smoothness to your writing. They also allow you to show a tight, exact relationship between two ideas. Versatile structures, these **compound sentences**!

# 22

## COMPOUND SENTENCES

## LEARN THEM!

**One twin *compounded* a felony and went behind the walls, AND the other twin *compounded* interest and went to Wall Street.**

*You may*

**compound** a felony (**add** to a crime by accepting a bribe not to prosecute the suspect) ... or ...

suffer from a **compound** fracture (when a broken bone tears soft tissue, creating an **additional** problem).

*You may*

prefer **compound** interest on your savings (interest on interest **added** to interest on principal) ... or ...

grow only **compound** flowers (**many** small flowers that appear to be a **single** bloom).

As you probably have deduced by now, **compound** refers to something that is made up of *two or more* parts.

Start easy—by looking at the **compound word:** a word made by *combining* two other words.

> Take the words "horse" and "laugh."
> Combine them.
> You get "horselaugh," a new word—one that describes a loud coarse laugh, rather like a horse's snort!

Work with five compound words. With each, try to figure out a logical definition by considering the meaning of the two parts.

**A. COMPOUND WORDS**

1. shoplifter: _____

2. gumshoe: _____

3. railroad: _____

4. skyscraper: _____

5. handkerchief: _____

(*Bonus:* This exercise should have added to your awareness of the meaning and power of words. Had you ever realized before that a skyscraper is a building so high that it seems to *scrape* the *sky?*)

**A HORSELAUGH**

Now consider the compound parts of a simple sentence. Remember: compound simply means having two or more parts.

■ It is possible to have a
**compound subject**
in a *simple* sentence:

[**Terri** and **Tim**] joined the circus.

Two subjects are connected by the conjunction **and**.

■ It is possible to have a
**compound verb**
in a *simple* sentence:

Tim [**antagonized** and **frightened**] the trained elephant.

Two verbs are connected by the conjunction **and**.

■ It is possible to have a
**compound object**
in a *simple* sentence:

Terri broke [**the trapeze bar** and **the trampoline.**]

Two objects are connected by the conjunction **and**.

■ It is even possible to have all three:
**a compound subject,**
**a compound verb,** and
**a compound object**
in a *simple* sentence:

[**Terri** and **Tim**] [**washed** and **dried**] [**the glasses** and **the china.**]

The important fact is that—regardless of the number of subjects, verbs, or objects—**each of the above sentences conveys *one* and only *one* complete thought.**

*Special Note:* **either ... or** and **neither ... nor** are pairs of conjunctions often used in compound parts. Examples:

[**Neither** Terri **nor** Tim] will put the dishes away.

The largest firework of all will be ignited by [**either** Terri **or** Tim.]

In the following sentences, bracket each compound part and then identify each as *compound subject*, *compound verb*, or *compound object*.

1. Meg and Harley were the noisiest surfers on the beach.

    _____

2. At the top of each wave, they shrieked and whistled.

    _____

3. One day their horrible noise split the eardrums and the patience of the lifeguard.

    _____

4. The lifeguard and her boss promptly reprimanded Meg and Harley and banned them from the beach and the ocean.

    _____

## C. COMPOUND SENTENCES

Finally, consider the **compound sentence.** Take any two simple sentences, connect them with a conjunction, and you have a compound sentence.

EXAMPLE: Tim antagonized and frightened the trained elephant,

**and**

Terri broke the trapeze bar and the trampoline.

The first simple sentence explains what Tim did to the elephants, and the second *simple* sentence explains what Terri did to the equipment. Two complete independent thoughts connected by the conjunction **and** form a *compound* sentence.

---

A **coordinating conjunction** is a conjunction that connects two equal and independent parts. The most common coordinating conjunctions are

**and     but     or.**

---

This may help you to remember them . . .

**And** may be considered a *plus* (+) sign.

**But** may be considered a *minus* (−) sign.

**Or** may be considered an *equal* (=) sign between two possibilities.

How do you decide which coordinating conjunction to use? Just apply a little common sense. Which is logical in a particular sentence? Try it—by supplying **coordinate** conjunctions for the following compound sentences.

**1.** Mary is going to China, _____ her sister is going with her.

**2.** Mary is going to China, _____ her sister is staying home.

**3.** Will Mary go to China, _____ will she stay home?

You see? It's not very difficult—if you keep your wits about you. Notice, too, that a comma is used *before* the coordinating conjunction in a compound sentence.

# 23

## COMPOUND SENTENCES
## USE THEM!

A *rolling* sentence—as undulating (wave-like) as a sweep of hills, as rhythmical as "America, the Beautiful." That's what you want when you write; that's what the compound sentence will help you to achieve.

In each of the following clusters, there are two or three short, choppy sentences. Combine them into a good *compound* sentence, using a coordinating conjunction (*and*, *but*, or *or*).

**A. COMBINING SENTENCES**

1. During their shopping expedition, Don bought three video game cartridges. Jan bought six LP records.

   _____

   _____

2. I have been a pilot for five years. I have never flown across the Atlantic Ocean.

   _____

   _____

3. Are you going to call Jason? Shall I?

   _____

4. The teacher lectured. Most of the students didn't take notes.

   _____

   _____

5. Ellen likes baseball. Her brother Tom likes football. Their sister Sue doesn't like any sports.

   _____

   _____

   _____

Why is it usually cool at a baseball game?

Because of all the fans.

(*Note:* did you remember to use a comma between the two parts of each *compound* sentence? Check. Add one if necessary.)

Each question or pair of questions below can be answered by using *one* compound sentence. In the first three, a coordinating conjunction is suggested. After that, you're on your own!

B. CREATING COMPOUND SENTENCES

1. Which food is your favorite? Which other food do you like almost as much? (coordinating conjunction: **and**)

   _____

   _____

2. You just won $50,000. List two alternative ways of spending it. (coordinating conjunction: **or**)

   _____

   _____

3. Name one country (other than the U.S.) in which you would like to live for a while. Why aren't you? (coordinating conjunction: **but**)

   _____

   _____

4. If traveling in a space rocket were made available to the public, would you like to visit the Moon? What one problem might prevent you?

   _____

   _____

5. List one sign of spring and one sign of autumn.

   _____

6. If you had the ability and the opportunity to learn *any* two skills, which would you like to master? (Examples: operating a computer, writing a novel, skiing.)

   _____

   _____

7. You have been invited to take part in an African safari. Accept or reject the invitation. Add a brief comment.

   _____

   _____

**SAFARI:** an expedition or journey, usually for hunting or exploring.

The rich used to use guns; today's tourists use cameras.

EXCURSION TO THE MOON $200 ROUND TRIP FARE

**8.** What animal makes a satisfying pet? What animal does not?

_____

_____

**9.** You and your brother decide to open a small car-washing business. Which jobs would you be willing to do? Which jobs would you not be willing to do?

_____

_____

**10.** Josie, Lauren, and Jennifer are going on a camping trip. What will each girl carry?

_____

_____

**C. PLAY A PROOFREADER**

Below is a short paragraph. Read it.

> ¹Cliff went for a hike. ²Mac went with him. ³They walked along the road for about two hours. ⁴They were tired. ⁵They were not exhausted. ⁶They decided to walk up a mountain. ⁷They didn't quite make it to the top. ⁸As it grew dark, they walked home, their legs tired and their feet sore.

Now give some vitality to the paragraph by following these directions.

**a.** Combine sentences 1 and 2, making a compound sentence.

_____

**b.** Line 2: add an adverb after the verb _walked_. _____

**c.** Line 2: change "the road" to the name of a specific road.

_____

**d.** Combine sentences 4 and 5, making a compound sentence.

_____

**e.** Line 4: replace the verb "walk (up)" with a more specific, more dramatic verb.

_____

**f.** Line 4: change "a mountain" to the name of a specific mountain.

_____

**g.** Combine sentences 6 and 7, making a compound sentence.

_____

**h.** Line 5: replace the verb "walked" with a more dramatic and specific verb.

_____

**i.** Line 6: replace the adjective "tired" with a stronger adjective.

_____

**j.** Line 6: replace the adjective "sore" with a stronger adjective.

_____

Now copy the _revised_ paragraph below.

_____

_____

_____

_____

_____

_____

_____

_____

_____

_____

| WORDS TO DESCRIBE A HIKE |
| --- |
| trudge |
| plod |
| aching |
| fatigued |
| march |
| tingling |
| mount |
| wearily |
| boldly |
| scale |
| blistered |
| briskly |
| chafe |
| crawl |
| climb |

Finally, read both paragraphs aloud, first the original and then the revised. Do you see the difference?

# 24

## COMPOUND SENTENCES
## USE THEM IN <u>YOUR</u> WRITING!

**A.** A **filler** is a short item—interesting or amusing—used in a magazine or a newspaper to fill a couple of inches of space. Below is a filler about the origin of "shaking hands." Read it.

> [1]We shake hands to greet someone. [2]We could touch feet, instead. [3]We could rub noses. [4]We could even bump heads. [5]There's a perfectly good reason for shaking hands. [6]In ancient times most males carried weapons. [7]Men who didn't know each other well were wary when they met. [8]They hesitated to get too close, since one might draw a knife or sword and stab the other. [9]So it became a custom for both men to put down their weapons. [10]They held forth empty hands to show good faith. [11]Soon the empty hands clasped. [12]The handshake was born.

Revise it. Make it tighter, more interesting. Try combining sentences. Try using different types of sentences. Work on scrap paper, and—after you have finished—return to this page.

\*     \*     \*     \*     \*     \*     \*

Here are some suggestions for revision. Check them against your own work. You may wish to incorporate some of them in your final revision.

**a.** Change sentence 1 to an interrogative sentence.

**b.** Combine sentences 2, 3, and 4 into a compound interrogative sentence.

**c.** Eliminate the prepositional phrase in #5.

**d.** Combine 6 and 7 into a compound sentence.

**e.** Combine 9 and 10 into one sentence, using a compound infinitive (*to* + a verb).

**f.** Combine 11 and 12 into a compound sentence.

Place a check mark next to each possible change (a to f) that you made *before* you read the above suggestions. Did you think of at least three on your own?

128

Remember: not everyone will revise the same piece of writing in the same way. There are dozens of possibilities, and the final decision, always, rests with *you*.

Finally—copy the revised filler below.

_____

_____

_____

_____

_____

_____

_____

_____

_____

_____

_____

---

*What you just revised is a paragraph of explanation. A paragraph of explanation starts with a generalization, then proceeds to a discussion of reasons that lead to the generalization. The generalization-to-explanation organization is similar to the generalization-to-details organization.*

---

**B.** Now it's your turn. The frankfurter is often called a "hot dog." Why?

DATA INPUT: The frankfurter: named after Frankfurt, Germany, where it originated.

The Polo Grounds, N.Y.C., 1900: Vendors shouted "Get your red hots!" They hoped to appeal to chilled customers on cold days.

A few years later: Ted Dorgan, a Hearst cartoonist, drew a picture of a stretched-out dachshund on a bun—reminding everyone of the frankfurter's German origin.

Coney Island, 1913: The term "hot dog" was banned. It was considered offensive.

In spite of the ban, the term "hot dog" soon became popular and is often used today.

Take the input. Remember that the purpose of this paragraph is to *explain* why the frankfurter is often called a "hot dog." Then write, using your revised paragraph about handshaking as a guide.

_____

_____

_____

_____

_____

_____

_____

_____

_____

_____

**C.** This time you're completely on your own. Start with a generalization that requires an explanation. Your generalization might be ...

    (a)  The most popular sport in our school is _____.

    (b)  Every student should (or should not) have at least one study period a day.

    (c)  Teenage fashions are unpopular with parents.

    (d)  _____ is an organization that helps young people to learn to handle the real world. (Fill the blank with—Boy Scouts, Girl Scouts, the 4-H, the FFA, or any other organized group.)

*Step 1:*  Choose your generalization carefully. Which one do you know the most about? Which one do you feel strongly about? This step is important. If you do not belong to an organization, you probably *shouldn't* choose "d." If you're an ardent soccer player, you probably *should* choose "a." So choose with care, and write your choice below.

_____

*Step 2:*  Now think about the generalization you chose. *Why* is it true?

    EXAMPLE:  (b)  Many boys and girls have chores to do at home. With a study hall, they can do some of their homework in school.

    EXAMPLE:  (d)  Students who belong to the FFA (Future Farmers of America) learn to judge animals, a useful skill when they themselves become farmers.

List below *three* reasons why *your* generalization is true.

_____

_____

_____

_____

_____

_____

*Step 3:* Write your paragraph of explanation, starting with a generalization and going on to explain that generalization. (Don't forget how useful the compound sentence can be!)

_____

_____

_____

_____

_____

_____

_____

_____

_____

_____

_____

_____

_____

_____

_____

_____

_____

**WRITING TECHNIQUE**

# 8

**Use compound sentences to vary the *rhythm* of your writing: short simple sentence followed by a longer compound sentence, and then a short simple sentence. This technique will make your writing smoother and more lively.**

# IF I HAD A MILLION DOLLARS . . .

## USE COMPLEX SENTENCES

THE NINTH STEP TO BETTER WRITING is to use **complex** sentences: sentences in which one part is dependent on another. A complex sentence allows you to show an exact relationship between two or more ideas.

> *"When you win, you're an old pro. When you lose, you're an old man."* (Charley Conerly)
>
> *"If you watch a game, it's fun. If you play it, it's recreation. If you work at it, it's golf."* (Bob Hope)
>
> *"Sport is hard work for which you do not get paid."* (Irvin S. Cobb)

Like compound sentences, complex sentences help you to eliminate short, choppy sentences and add smoothness and rhythm to your writing. You may find them tricky at first, but once you have mastered them, you will find them invaluable allies.

# 25

## COMPLEX SENTENCES
## LEARN THEM!

You want to learn to drive, but—

*First:* you have to persuade your parents that you are old enough and mature enough;

*Second:* you have to find the money for a learner's permit;

*Third:* you have to acquire a learner's permit;

*Fourth:* you have to find someone to teach you.

So—before you can learn to drive, you have to do *four* things; and some of those four depend on others. For example, the third depends on the second: you cannot acquire a learner's permit until you have the necessary money.

In short, if you want to learn to drive, you are faced with a **complex** situation: a situation made up of several parts, at least one of which is dependent on another.

In the same way, a **complex** sentence has two parts, one of which is dependent on another.

## A. FINISH THE THOUGHT

Your friend meets you at the gym door and invites you to jet to Paris with her the next day for lunch on the Champs Élysées. You answer:

I will go. . .

So far, everything is simple and clear. Then you remember your science class and you add:

. . . IF I complete my science homework tonight.

The words you added— "IF I complete my science homework tonight"—is a **dependent** clause. Read it aloud. It doesn't make sense without an **independent** clause on which to depend.

The complete sentence—"I will go IF I complete my science homework tonight"—is a **complex** sentence, made up of an independent clause and a dependent clause.

Another example:

Jason cried [when his leg broke.]

"When his leg broke" doesn't make sense by itself. We ask: "Well, what happened when his leg broke?" The answer lies in the main or independent clause: "Jason cried."

---

A **clause** is a group of words having a subject and a verb. A **dependent clause,** although it contains a subject and a verb, cannot stand alone and make sense. It depends on an **independent clause** for its meaning.

<u>When Joan smiles,</u> <u>her eyes glow.</u>
    *dependent clause*     *independent clause*

<u>Louise wore a beautiful gown</u> <u>that her mother had made.</u>
    *independent clause*     *dependent clause*

---

Practice writing complex sentences by adding a dependent clause to each of the following independent clauses. To help you, we've provided a suitable **subordinate conjunction.**

**1.** Millicent hit a homer **because** _____

_____

**2.** Everyone will vote for you for class president **if** _____

_____

**3.** Four-year-old Timmy smashed his tricycle **when** _____

_____

**4.** Max devoured two whole pizzas **although** _____

_____

(Be careful with the next one. Don't use **after** as a preposition, as in the phrase, "after dinner." To have a dependent clause, you must add a subject and a verb.)

**5.** I'll have a banana split **after** _____

_____

Of course, dependent clauses do not have to come at the end of a sentence. They can come at the beginning:

[**Before** it stopped snowing,] drifts ten feet high had accumulated.

. . . or, in the middle:

He walked, [**as** he had planned,] to the shopping plaza.

**B. AT THE BEGINNING. . .**

135

Some more practice. Add a dependent clause to each of the following independent clauses. In each case, a suitable subordinate conjunction has been provided.

1. **If** _____,

   I will give you a million dollars.

2. **When** _____,

   she jumped for joy.

3. The automobile, **after** _____,

   was a total wreck.

4. The monster, **before** _____,

   smiled sweetly.

5. **Because** _____,

   you will be grounded for three months.

**C. RECOGNITION TIME**

This time your task is easy. In each of the following sentences, place brackets around the dependent clause and underline the subordinate conjunction.

*Example:* Tillie kissed her little brother [<u>when</u> he handed her his piggy bank.]

1. If you win the lottery, will you take a trip around the world?

   (Yes, even interrogative sentences can be complex!)

2. Scott was skiing down Prospect Mountain when he came face to face with a grizzly bear.

3. Although Cari had studied non-stop for 72 hours, she failed the test.

4. The duck, after it bit the cow, waddled away with dignity.

5. He loved dinosaurs until he met one.

---

## Comments on Commas

- Use a comma at the end of a **dependent** clause that begins a sentence. (See number 1 above.)

- Do not use a comma at the end of an **independent** clause that starts a sentence. (See number 2 above.)

- Use two commas to set off a **dependent** clause that comes in the middle of a complex sentence **if** the dependent clause could be omitted without changing the meaning of the sentence. (See number 4 above.)

---

**D. STAR-STUDDED SENTENCES**

The stars speak. . . Unfortunately, some of the dependent clauses have wandered away, leaving fractured sentences. Your task is to use each of the dependent clauses below in one of the fractured sentences that follow them. Be alert—you will need common sense and imagination, as well as grammar, to make the sentences whole again!

- if someone is dumb enough to offer me a million dollars to make a picture
- if you haven't got charity in your heart
- that people will look at anything rather than each other
- unless he's Humphrey Bogart
- until they can be made unbreakable
- when I was three and unknown
- where an individual has the opportunity to go from nothing to something
- who said talk is cheap

1. "_____,
   you have the worst kind of heart trouble." (*Bob Hope*)

2. "America has always meant to me one of the few places in the world _____
   _____." (*Phyllis Diller*)

3. "A guy who twitches his lips is just another guy with a lip twitch—_____."
   (*Sammy Davis, Jr.*)

4. "I remember _____."
   (*Shirley Temple*)

5. "Hearts will never be practical _____
   _____." (*"The Wizard of Oz"*)

6. "Television has proved _____
   _____." (*Ann Landers*)

7. "_____
   _____,
   I am certainly not dumb enough to turn it down." (*Elizabeth Taylor*)

8. "The man _____
   never hired a lawyer." (*Charles Bronson*)

# 26

## COMPLEX SENTENCES
## USE THEM!

Tight and clear—that's what you want your writing to be, and that's what you will achieve **if** you use **complex** sentences. Practice!

**Coordinate** conjunctions (**and, but, or**) connect independent clauses.

**Subordinate** conjunctions connect an independent clause and a dependent clause.

Some common subordinate conjunctions:

| | | |
|---|---|---|
| after | if | when |
| although | since | where |
| as | that | which |
| because | unless | while |
| before | until | who |

Combine the sentences in each of the following clusters into one good **complex** sentence by using a suitable **subordinate conjunction**. (See the list above.)

**A. COMBINING SENTENCES**

1. The hunter spotted the deer. He raised his rifle.

   _____

   _____

2. She checked over her mountain-climbing equipment. Then she started up the Matterhorn.

   _____

   _____

3. Her pet alligator died. She cried for weeks.

   _____

   _____

**4.** Soaring across the sky in a hot-air balloon is a fascinating experience. You should try it.

_____

_____

**5.** I was watching a terrifying star wars movie. An explosion rocked the house.

_____

_____

A complex sentence may have two—or more—dependent clauses, as you will see below.

**6.** Frank lost a tennis ball. He had no mittens or hat or jacket. He still plunged into a snowdrift to find the ball.

_____

_____

_____

**7.** The Martian smiled. The Earthling trembled. She knew the alien planned to kidnap her.

_____

_____

**8.** I foolishly left the main road. I found myself in a swamp. The swamp was full of alligators and mammoth mosquitoes.

_____

_____

_____

**9.** The toddlers' world consists mostly of adults. These adults must seem like giants. These adults tower above them.

_____

_____

_____

**10.** The petrel is a seabird. It flies along the tops of waves. It appears to be walking on water.

_____

_____

Below are ten "baby" sentences—sentences of two or three words. "Flesh out" each one by adding a descriptive, detailed dependent clause.

*Example:* I panicked.

**When the dinosaur loomed above me,** I panicked.

I panicked **until I saw Superman swoop down from the sky.**

**After I beat off the twenty intruders,** I panicked.

Use your imagination! Be as amusing as you like. . . and use as many different subordinate conjunctions as possible.

I cried
   (no comma)
       when I fell.

BUT . . .

When I fell,
   (comma)
       I cried.

1. I cried bitterly.

   _____

   _____

2. Edwin laughed gleefully.

   _____

   _____

3. I cannot answer.

   _____

   _____

4. You will fail.

   _____

   _____

5. Brenda slapped him.

   _____

   _____

6. I won't go.

   _____

   _____

7. Daniel is moody.

   _____

   _____

8. Lilybell pouted.

   _____

   _____

**9.** Oliver collapsed.

_____

_____

**10.** The spectators applauded.

_____

_____

Here is another rather dull paragraph. The short simple sentences are boring. The drab words are boring. Read—and be bored. . .

C. PLAY A PROOFREADER

> [1]Jenny walked up to the town bully. [2]She took off her glasses. [3]"You've been asking for this," she said. [4]"You're bigger than anyone else. [5]You think you're better than anyone else. [6]You're not!" [7]She took his arm. [8]She threw him over her shoulder. [9]He landed in a pigpen. [10]He began to cry. [11]The pigs were eating. [12]He disturbed them. [13]The pigs disliked him. [14]They pushed him deeper into the mud. [15]"That's that," said Jenny. [16]She put on her glasses. [17]She smiled. [18]She walked away.

Now revise the paragraph, following these instructions.

**Step 1: combine sentences for variety and smoothness**

**a.** Combine sentences 1 and 2 into a complex sentence.

_____

_____

**b.** Combine sentences 4 and 5 into a complex sentence.

_____

_____

**c.** Combine sentences 7 and 8 into a simple sentence with a compound verb.

_____

_____

**d.** Combine sentences 9 and 10 into a complex sentence.

_____

_____

**e.** Combine sentences 11, 12, and 13 into one complex sentence, using two dependent clauses.

_____

_____

_____

**f.** Combine sentences 16, 17, and 18 into one simple sentence with a compound verb.

_____

_____

_____

## Step 2: replace drab words with colorful words

**a.** (_line 1_) Replace the verb "walked (up)" with a more specific, more dramatic verb.

a _____

**b.** (_line 1_) Replace the verb "took (off)" with a better verb.

b _____

**c.** (_line 2_) Replace the verb "asking" with a stronger verb.

c _____

**d.** (_line 2_) Add a suitable adverb after the verb "said."

d _____

**e.** (_line 4_) Replace the verb "took" with a stronger verb.

e _____

**f.** (_line 4_) Replace the verb "threw" with a more dramatic verb.

f _____

**g.** (_line 5_) Replace the verb "cry" with a stronger verb.

g _____

**h.** (_line 7_) Replace the noun "mud" with a more graphic noun.

h _____

---

### STRONG VERBS

seize
snarl
remove
whimper
whine
moan
stride
amble
tiptoe
wail
strut
plead
rob
grasp
grab

---

**i.** (*line 8*) Add an appropriate adverb to modify "smiled."  i _____

**j.** (*line 8*) Replace the verb "walked" with a stronger verb.  j _____

Now copy the revised paragraph on the lines below. Then read the original paragraph aloud. Next read the revised paragraph aloud. Can you *hear* the difference—not only in dramatic effectiveness but in rhythm?

_____

_____

_____

_____

_____

_____

_____

_____

_____

_____

_____

_____

_____

_____

_____

_____

_____

_____

_____

_____

_____

_____

_____

**VIDERE** (Latin) to *see*

**VIDEO** the *visual* portion of television

**REVISION** to *see* again, or to *look* over again, in order to correct or improve

# 27

## COMPLEX SENTENCES

## USE THEM IN <u>YOUR</u> WRITING!

**A.** Most kids dream of getting into the Guinness *Book of World Records*. To do so, you must do something better or longer than anyone else. For example, an Australian punched a ball for over 125 hours; five high school majorettes twirled for 44 hours; and a girl in California blew a Bubble Yum bubble 17 inches in diameter. What can *you* do? What record might you be able to set? Think for a minute. Then write below the activity you will pursue in order to get into the *Book of World Records*. (Be as wild as you like; after all, you're *writing* about it, not *doing* it!)

Ready? Now pretend you have already accomplished your purpose. Before you begin writing about *your* experience, read the paragraph below. After that, describe how *you* set an unusual World Record. Organize the paragraph by moving from a generalization to supporting details; OR from details to a generalization.

When I started sitting on a tower of twenty bricks on Saturday, April 4th, I little realized what the result would be. I did it because I was bored—and because I wondered if it could be done. It was uncomfortable; after all, a brick is hard, has sharp edges, and is rather small for the human posterior. Within thirty minutes a gang of little kids gathered around me, asking questions and giggling. Soon older kids joined them, and then some adults. Hours passed. A rainstorm cooled me off but also soaked me. A pigeon sat on my head. During the night only a couple of people stayed to encourage me. After 34 hours and 23 minutes, I fell asleep and fell off the tower of bricks. But I had lasted long enough to set a world record!

_____

_____

_____

_____

_____

_____

_____

_____

_____

_____

_____

_____

_____

_____

_____

_____

_____

_____

**B.** A *tour de force* is a French phrase that has become part of our English language. It means—an act of great skill or strength or ingenuity. Some time ago an author wrote an entire novel without using the letter "e." Now *that* is a tour de force! Your challenge? A much smaller tour de force: to write a paragraph explaining *why* teenagers are so often rebellious—and to do it using *only* complex sentences! Is it possible? Can it be done? Try!

_____

_____

_____

_____

_____

_____

_____

_____

_____

_____

ANOTHER
*TOUR
DE FORCE*

Victor Hugo, the French novelist, wrote one of the longest sentences ever published. It was 823 words long and filled three pages!

**C.** A new, incredibly fantastic amusement park has just opened near your home. Invite a friend to visit it with you. But first—make a few notes. . .

What is the name of this park? (Make up a good one!)

_____

What rides or activities would interest your friend and make her or him wish to go with you? (List three.)

_____

_____

_____

_____

_____

_____

When would you go? What date? What time?

_____

_____

Will you meet your friend at the park? At home? Where?

_____

_____

This is your *input*, the data you need before you invite your friend. Now write a letter to your friend. Write it in such a way that your friend will be eager to accept. Check page 44 for the correct format for a friendly letter. Then write it—on scrap paper. When you have finished, read it over. Ask yourself the questions we have been asking: are the verbs vivid? The sentences varied? etcetera, etcetera, etcetera.

After you have made any corrections or improvements, copy the final draft of your letter below.

_____
_____
_____
_____
_____
_____
_____
_____
_____
_____
_____
_____
_____
_____
_____
_____
_____
_____
_____
_____
_____
_____

WRITING TECHNIQUE

# 9

Use complex sentences to vary the rhythm of your writing and to make clear the relationships between ideas. Use them to help you say exactly what you want to say!

# WRITING TIME—III

**A. "FLESHING OUT" EXERCISES**

Just to your right is a magic window. Through it you see a girl . . .

**A young female swimmer stands at the edge of the pool. Her right ankle is tightly strapped.**

Who is she? What happened to her ankle? Why is she going swimming? How does she feel? Use the answers to these questions to "flesh out" the sentences—to make them come alive.

Fifteen-year-old Debbie Allen froze at the edge of the pool, bitterly aware of her tightly strapped right ankle. "Go ahead and swim," her doctor had said, "but swim slowly." A thousand miles away her three partners were preparing for the swimming relay race with visions of an Olympic Gold dancing in their heads. An Olympic Gold! She shook her head fiercely and raised her arms above her head. In four years, she promised herself . . . in four years . . .

Of course this is just one scenario. It could be quite different. The girl could be Jemina Lane who has a bone disease and is swimming in a desperate attempt to strengthen her bones and muscles. *Or*—she could be Sylvia Mather who wants to be a ballet dancer and is swimming to strengthen a weak ankle. *Or*—she could be Jennifer O'Hare whose right ankle was nipped by a shark a week ago and who is now trying to overcome her new fear of water.

"Fleshing out" can be fun. It gives you a chance to use your imagination and to develop all sorts of weird story lines. Practice—by turning each cluster of sentences (next page) into a well-developed paragraph—and do it by adding dramatic details.

"A novelist writes, as a painter paints, with eyes rather than hands."

**Christopher Derrick**

1. **A young man walks out of the house carrying skis.** Who is he? Where is he going? Is he a new skier, or an experienced one? How does he feel? Does he have any fears?

*Your exciting scenario:*

_____

_____

_____

_____

_____

_____

_____

_____

_____

_____

2. **A man and a woman raised their rifles as a large animal emerged from the jungle.** (Ask yourself some questions; answer them; write.)

*Your exciting scenario:*

_____

_____

_____

_____

_____

_____

_____

_____

_____

_____

Are you beginning to see the power of words? With the right words rightly used, you can express what *you* think, what *you* feel. And that is—power.

Here is a paragraph about an interesting human event, but it is written in a dull, uninspired style. Your assignment? To rewrite the article. You may add words, combine sentences, change sentence order. In other words, you may make any changes you like, but you must keep the basic facts as they are given. See if you can turn this dull story into an interesting one. (Option: if you like, you may make up one or two quotations to use in the story.)

A man named Jerry Greene lives in Boise, Idaho. His wife's name is Catharine. Two years ago the Greenes went to Niagara Falls, New York, on a vacation trip. Greene lost his wallet. The wallet contained $10,000. This was all the money he owned. Last week his wallet was returned. A ten-year-old girl found it. The girl's name is Ellie Drew. She found it in some tall grass on the Three Sisters, a tiny island near the Falls. She sent the wallet to the Greenes. They thanked her and sent her $200. The Greenes were happy to have their money back.

**PAINT WITH YOUR EYES!**

*See* Niagara Falls.
*See* the Greenes losing their money.
*See* Ellie finding it.
SEE—and

**PAINT WITH YOUR EYES!**

Some suggestions:

- You may want to start with a one-sentence description of Niagara Falls as seen by Catharine and Jerry Greene just before Greene realizes he has lost his wallet.
- You may want to start with Ellie finding the wallet and thinking of all she could do with $10,000.

*You* decide—how to start it, how to develop it, how to conclude it.

Write your revised version below.

_____

_____

_____

_____

_____

_____

_____

_____

_____

_____

_____

_____

Finished? Read it over. Is it fast-moving? Does it use specific nouns and action verbs? If not, go back to work. When it sounds good, go on to . . .

Read the following information. (It's true!)

The Hard Crab Derby is the highlight of the Crab Bowl.

The Crab Bowl is held annually on Labor Day Weekend.

The Crab Bowl is held in Crisfield, Maryland.

The Hard Crab Derby is a competitive race.

The participants are hard-shell crabs.

Each crab has a number painted on its back.

The crabs are lined up on a wooden track.

The track is 15 feet long and slanted.

A starting gun gives the signal for the race to start.

The crabs move along the wooden track.

Their owners cheer for them.

In 1982 Compromise won the race and the title "King Crab."

One Crab Derby fan said that the prize for the winning crab is that "He don't get et."

1. Use the above information to write a brief and amusing newspaper story. Use any type of organization you like. (Work on scrap paper.)

2. Read your story. Is it lively? Clear? Have you used strong action verbs? A few startling adjectives? Have you used different kinds of sentence structure: simple, compound, and complex? Revise. Replace. Add. Then copy your revised paragraphs below.

_____

_____

_____

_____

_____

_____

_____

_____

_____

_____

_____

_____

_____

_____

_____

VICHYSSOISE,
A THICK,
CREAMY
POTATO
SOUP ...

USE
APPOSITIVES

THE TENTH STEP TO BETTER WRITING is to use **appositives**:
phrases that describe or explain nouns or pronouns.
Appositives *describe* a person, *define* an unusual word
(see the title of this unit), *identify* a place, or *explain* a
process.

---

**FROM THE WORLD OF ADVERTISING**

**Wheaties,** *the Breakfast of Champions* . . .

**Coca-Cola,** *the pause that refreshes* . . .

**Miracle Whip,** *the bread spread* . . .

**Mighty Dog,** *the pure beef brand* . . .

---

With appositives, you can compress two sentences into
one—faster than we can describe the process! Experiment
with them. You will find them useful—frequently; and an
aid to writing—always.

# 28

## APPOSITIVES

## LEARN THEM!

What is an **appositive?** The easiest way to define it is to illustrate it.

> E.T., [an alien], captured the hearts of the American people.
>
> ("An alien" is an appositive: it *identifies* E.T.)
>
> The biggest bluefin tuna, [a 1496-pound fish], was caught off Nova Scotia in 1979.
>
> ("A 1496-pound fish" is an appositive: it *describes* the tuna.)
>
> She ordered vichyssoise, [a thick, creamy potato soup usually served cold].
>
> ("A thick, creamy potato soup usually served cold" is an appositive: it *defines* vichyssoise.)

An **appositive** is a noun that tells something about a preceding noun.

I admire my <u>teacher</u>, [Mrs. Brown].
*appositive*

A noun in apposition usually has modifiers. Such a word-group, or **appositive phrase**, acts as a second noun.

I admire <u>Mrs. Brown</u>, [my teacher of English].
*appositive phrase*

An appositive *identifies* or *defines* or *describes* the noun that it follows.

1. Some appositives *identify* a person, place, or thing.

Swahili, [the language of East Africa], is spoken by 32 million people. (The appositive, "the language of East Africa," *identifies* Swahili.)

Eugenie Clark, [a well-known marine biologist], has taught sharks to recognize different colors and designs. (The appositive, "a well-known marine biologist," *identifies* Eugenie Clark.)

Bracket the appositive in each of the following sentences and draw an arrow to the word or phrase that it *identifies*.

a. Mandarin, China's national language, is spoken by 726 million people.

b. The major language of the Western world, English, is spoken by 397 million people.

c. Maria decided to write about Hawaii, the fiftieth state to be admitted to the Union.

d. Hetty Green, a miserly millionaire, wore ragged clothing and lived in cheap rented rooms.

e. Rube Goldberg, the wildly imaginative inventor and cartoonist, introduced the word "baloney" to the English language.

2. Some appositives *define* a person, place, or thing.

The crowd applauded for the funambulist, [a tightrope walker]. (The appositive, "a tightrope walker," *defines* "funambulist.")

She decided to study campanology, [the art of ringing bells]. (The appositive, "the art of ringing bells," *defines* "campanology.")

**A victim of
AILUROPHOBIA.**

Bracket the appositive in each of the following sentences and draw an arrow to the word or phrase it *defines*.

a. Napoleon Bonaparte suffered from ailurophobia, the fear of cats.

b. A just-born vicuna, a llama-like animal of the Andes, can run faster than a human being.

c. Bamboo, tropical grass with hollow woody stems, sometimes grows three feet in twenty-four hours.

d. Thousands of schoolchildren today are mastering Logo, a new electronic-age language.

e. The construction worker ordered a BLT, a bacon, lettuce, and tomato sandwich.

3. Some appositives *describe* a person, place, or thing.

The ostrich egg, [the largest bird egg in the modern world], is from six to eight inches long. (The appositive, "the largest bird egg in the modern world," *describes* "ostrich egg.")

In 1976, Clarence Dailey of Wisconsin grew the world's largest tomato, [a six-pound, eight-ounce monster]. (The appositive, "a six-pound, eight-ounce monster," *describes* "tomato.")

Bracket the appositive in each of the following sentences and draw an arrow to the word or phrase it *describes*.

a. The cradle gym, a colorful contraption designed to amuse babies, was invented by the American Indian.

b. Maryanne, a platinum blonde, was the belle of the party.

c. After living in New York for twenty years, he moved to Iowa, a corn-growing state.

**d.** They finally hired Giovanni, a tall, six-foot redhead, for the lead role.

**e.** In England we visited the Tower of London, a prison for princes.

**B. PLAY A WORD DETECTIVE**

Below is a list of *appositives*. Notice that some are quite long.

- a brief period right after the election when almost everyone admires him
- a month-long period of happiness
- a popular drink in Old England
- a young man and a young woman
- actually "eating money"
- an adjective now used to describe the gown and the ceremony
- preferably the English classroom
- the study of language, especially of the Greek and Latin languages
- uneducated people who were often superstitious
- usually Italian or Spanish or French
- usually the wife but sometimes the husband

Now use your common sense and general knowledge to place each of the above appositives in one of the blanks below.

1. Centuries ago, every bride was toasted with ale, _____ _____. With time, the "bride's ale" was shortened to "bridal"—_____ _____.

2. You want "glamor"? The best place to acquire it is in the classroom, _____.

   For "glamor" comes from "grammar," _____ _____.

   The masses, _____,
   looked with awe at the students of "grammar" and suspected them of casting spells. Over the years the spelling changed, and today the young woman with "glamor" casts a different kind of spell!

3. When two people, _____,
   talk of "romance," they're actually dabbling in literature, for

---

**MNEMONIC AID**
To remember how to spell "grammar"—the first syllable contains a "ram" and the second syllable spells "ram" backwards.

157

a "romance" was originally a story of love told in a Romance language, _____ .

4. The word "aliment" means "food." That's why, after a divorce, one partner,_____ _____ , will ask the court to award "alimony," _____ .

5. A honeymoon,_____ _____ , owes its origin to the length of the moon-cycle. It once referred only to the short period following a marriage, but today even the President of the United States has a political honeymoon—_____ _____ .

*Bonus*: As you learned **appositives,** you also learned the origins of some common words. Fascinating, aren't they?

> BONUS something extra;
> something unexpected.
>
> From Latin *bonus,*
> meaning "good."

# 29

## APPOSITIVES

## USE THEM!

Appositives are compact, constructive, and concise. They may also be caustic or creative, cruel or crisp. But they are always worth cultivating! (Notice the alliteration.)

In each of the following clusters, there are two or more short choppy sentences. Combine them into one or two good sentences, as directed, by using an appositive.

### Example: Combine into one sentence:

*Short, Choppy:* Baboons are large African primates with dog-like muzzles. Egyptians trained baboons to act as waiters.

(Cancel repetition of *baboons*.)

*Combined:* Baboons, large African primates with dog-like muzzles, were trained by Egyptians to act as waiters.

(The appositive phrase, set off by two commas, describes *baboons*.)

YOUR TURN: (Combine into one sentence.)

**A. COMBINING SENTENCES**

1. James Buchanan was the only bachelor to serve as President of the United States. He was elected in 1856.

   _____

   _____

2. Philadelphia is the city of "Brotherly Love." It owes its name to the Greek word "philos" which means "love" and to the Greek word "adelphos" which means "brother."

   _____

   _____

   _____

**Philadelphia, "The City of Brotherly Love," is the home of the Liberty Bell.**

159

**3.** Beethoven was a world-famous musician. He composed most of his great symphonies after he became deaf.

_____

_____

**4.** Rats are carriers of disease. They have probably been responsible for more deaths than all the wars of history.

_____

_____

**5.** The Empire State Building is the second largest building in New York City. It was made with ten million bricks.

_____

_____

### Example:   Combine into two sentences:

*Short, Choppy:* Pikes Peak is 14,110 feet high. It is one of the highest peaks of the Rocky Mountains. It was named after Zebulon Montgomery Pike. Pike was captain of a small military band that "discovered" the peak in 1806.

*Combined:* Pikes Peak, one of the highest peaks of the Rocky Mountains, is 14,110 feet high. It was named after Zebulon Montgomery Pike, captain of a small military band that "discovered" the peak in 1806.

> (The first appositive, set off by two commas, describes *Pikes Peak*. The second appositive, set off by one comma, identifies Zebulon Montgomery Pike.)

YOUR TURN:

**6.** James Madison was the fourth President of the United States. He was also the smallest. Madison was only 5'4" tall and weighed less than a hundred pounds. He was a Virginian. (Combine into two sentences.)

_____

_____

_____

_____

7. In the Midwest in the 1880s, some towns forbade the sale of ice cream sodas on Sunday. Sunday was the Lord's Day. A clever storeowner skipped the soda and served a "Sunday soda." A "Sunday soda" was just ice cream and syrup. Eventually the name was shortened to "sundae." (Combine into three sentences, using the last one, as it is, as sentence 3.)

_____

_____

_____

8. The chewing gum that has been around the longest is Black Jack. Black Jack is a licorice-flavored gum. Another interesting gum is a sour-pickle flavored concoction. This is mildly popular in Japan. (Combine into two sentences.)

_____

_____

_____

9. Bob Hope is one of the most popular people in show business. He was once a prizefighter. Desi Arnaz is a successful actor-director. He was once a cleaner of bird cages. (Combine into two sentences.)

_____

_____

_____

10. Failure isn't permanent. John F. Kennedy was the popular 35th President of the United States. He lost by a landslide when he ran for president of his freshman class. Lucille Ball is the much-loved star of the "I Love Lucy" series. She was told she had no acting ability when she applied to a drama school. (Keep the first sentence as it is. Combine the other sentences into two.)

_____

_____

_____

Each sentence below is already correct and complete, but each will be more informative, more dramatic, if an appositive is added.

**Example: Last year I visited Germany, _____.**

One obvious appositive: a country in Europe

Other less obvious but better appositives:
the home of the Black Forest
a country that fascinates me
the home of knockwurst and sauerkraut

Said the Silly Student:

"Chicago is almost at the bottom of Lake Michigan."

What did the Silly Student say?

What did the Silly Student mean?

YOUR TURN: Add one clever or amusing appositive to each of the following sentences.

1. Last year I visited Chicago, _____

_____.

2. Millicent Manning, _____,
strode into the theater and terrified the eighty spectators.

3. My favorite dessert, _____,
makes me feel ten years younger and ten pounds heavier.

4. At the zoo, I stood for an hour watching the antics of my

favorite animal, _____.

5. If you wish to become healthier and smarter, spend two hours

daily on my hobby, _____.

6. Two silver birches, _____,

flank the main gate to the estate.

7. The soldier, _____,

challenged the six intruders.

8. "Kiss me or kill me!" said the lizard to the fair princess,

_____.

9. _____,

the roses transformed the old shack into a miniature castle.

10. If I were giving out awards, I'd give the top award to my

favorite TV program, _____.

162

Below is a short paragraph . . . marred by short choppy sentences. Read it.

My brother is a four-year-old electronic game champ. He twiddles the joysticks as though he had been doing it for twenty years. Like a miniature guru, he sits crosslegged in front of our TV set. The TV is the lair of dozens of exciting games. He inserts his favorite cartridge. His favorite cartridge is *Asteroids*. His eyes are gleaming orbs of anticipation. They glitter. He starts to play, gleefully manipulating the joysticks. The joysticks are twin tools to bliss. Five hours later he has racked up a fine score. He has accumulated a million points. My mother comes home, turns off the TV, and pulls the joysticks from his small, numb hands. "Enough, Einstein," she says firmly as she picks him up. "It's time for your nap."

The above paragraph contains *fifteen* sentences. Your assignment is to reduce the number to *nine*—and to do this by using appositives to combine some of the sentences. Remember:

---

An appositive is separated from the rest of the sentence: by *two* commas if the appositive falls within the sentence, *one* comma if the appositive ends the sentence.

---

Your revision . . .

_____

_____

_____

_____

_____

_____

_____

_____

_____

_____

_____

[*continued*]

_____

_____

_____

_____

_____

_____

_____

_____

_____

_____

_____

_____

_____

Read the original paragraph aloud. Read the revised paragraph aloud. Convinced—that appositives make a difference?

# 30

## APPOSITIVES

## USE THEM IN **YOUR** WRITING!

All good things come three by three, as you will see!

**A. 1.** The following paragraph has an introductory sentence and a concluding sentence, but no body.

Three People Who Changed My Life

Three people have changed the course of my life. _____

_____

_____

_____

_____

_____

_____

_____

_____

Years will pass, but even when I'm old, I'll remember these three "life-changing" friends!

Your job? To write three sentences, each with an appositive, that will make up the body of the paragraph.

> a teacher?
> a doctor?
> a clergyman?
> a favorite aunt or
>    uncle?
> a stranger?
> a celebrity?
> a brother or sister?
> a parent?
> a cashier?
> a police officer?
>   ?  ?  ?  ?

EXAMPLE: Mindy Johnson, *a short, plump brunette*, taught me how to spell—and saved me from failure in fourth grade. Mike Browne, *a ten-year-old, muscle-bound towhead*, punched me regularly until I learned to fight back. And Ellie Macintosh, *a bewitching little minx*, gave me my first kiss!

**2.** This next paragraph also has an introductory sentence and a conclusion, but no body.

Three Places I Will Never Forget

Many places leave their mark on those who live or visit there, but—for me—three places tower over all the rest. _____

_____

_____

_____

_____

_____

_____

_____

_____

_____

_____

_____

_____

_____

_____

Shopping malls?
Niagara Falls?

China's Great Wall?
A produce stall?

Kalamazoo?
Fifth Avenue?

A Chicago street?
A field of wheat?

Kennebunk, Maine?
Or Lake Champlain?

or WHERE?

These three places have moulded me, shaped me, prepared me for the rest of my life.

Again, your job is to write three sentences, each with an appositive, that will make up the body of the paragraph.

EXAMPLE: The Grand Canyon, *a majestic, rock-bound, ever-changing abyss*, taught me the beauty and grandeur of nature. (Only one example is given this time.)

**3.** The last (of the three) paragraphs has *no* introductory sentence, *no* conclusion, and *no* body. Your job is to write the complete paragraph—using the title as your only guide.

Some possibilities: the *one* time you earned 100 on a spelling test; the time you were on a winning team; the time you had an argument with your mother and she admitted you were right.

Three Times I Tasted Success

_____

_____

_____

_____

_____

_____

_____

_____

_____

_____

_____

_____

_____

_____

_____

_____

_____

_____

_____

_____

**B.** Combine appositives and contrasts to create sentences that are packed with information and drama.

> Michael Jackson, *a professional pop singer with a jeweled glove,* captures our dollars, but Jenny Jackson, *Tri-High's own blues crooner,* snares our hearts.

Notice that the two appositives provide contrasting pictures. You try it.

1.  **Try it with houses.**

    EXAMPLE: My first home, *a rat-infested, two-room flat in a Boston slum,* makes me appreciate my present home, *a twenty-room Colonial on Long Island Sound.*

    YOUR TURN:

    _____

    _____

    _____

2.  **Try it with people.**

    EXAMPLE: Who would be my escort to the prom—Tom, *tall, blond, and a klutz;* or Eric, *shorter, studious, and a fantastic dancer?*

    YOUR TURN:

    _____

    _____

    _____

3.  **Try it with toys or gadgets.**

    EXAMPLE: Much to her mother's horror, Samantha swapped a teddy bear, *an expensive import from Australia,* for a flying saucer, *a plastic gadget one can buy for $1.29 at any general store.*

    YOUR TURN:

    _____

    _____

    _____

    _____

**C.** This time try writing a complete paragraph, using the **comparison/ contrast** method of organization. (*Comparison* = pointing out similarities; *contrast* = pointing out differences).

When writing a comparison/contrast paragraph, start with a problem; discuss similarities; point out differences; draw a conclusion. First read the paragraph below. Next tackle the three exercises that follow. If possible, use a couple of appositives to strengthen your case.

> Which sport should be declared *the* national sport of the United States—swimming or skiing? Both strengthen muscles and improve coordination. Both are competitive, and both are fun. But there the similarities end. Skiing, *a sport for the rich*, demands expensive equipment, professional lessons, and transportation to often-remote skiing areas; while swimming, *a sport for the masses*, can be done anywhere—in a river or a lake or a backyard pool—and the only expense is a swimsuit. If only one of these sports can be chosen as *the* national sport, I vote emphatically for—swimming!

**1.** Which game should be declared the national game of the United States? (Some possibilities: chess, checkers, Monopoly, Trivial Pursuit, etc.) Nominate *two*.

_____ and _____

List similarities between the two games.

_____

_____

_____

_____

_____

List differences between the two games.

_____

_____

_____

_____

_____

— • —

**Allie and Alfie both like gum,
Both play checkers,
Both play a drum.**

**but**

**Allie is short, and Alfie is tall,
So Allie plays marbles
And Alfie basketball.**

— • —

Now write a comparison/contrast paragraph about the two games, ending with a conclusion based on your arguments.

_____

_____

_____

_____

_____

_____

_____

_____

_____

_____

_____

_____

2. Which sandwich should be declared the national sandwich of the United States? Nominate *two*.

_____ and _____

On scrap paper, list similarities and differences.

Write a comparison/contrast paragraph.

_____

_____

_____

_____

_____

_____

_____

_____

_____

_____

_____

_____

The SANDWICH: born on August 6, 1762, at 5 a.m.

John Montague, Earl of Sandwich, loved gambling, but he loved food, too. Once, during a 24-hour stay at the gaming table, he ordered a servant to bring him meat placed between two slices of bread so that he could eat without interrupting the game.

And so the SANDWICH came into existence.

**3.** Which animal should be declared the national animal of the United States? Nominate *two*.

_____ and _____

On scrap paper, list similarities and differences.

Write a comparison/contrast paragraph.

| grizzly bear |
| elephant |
| hippopotamus |
| giraffe |
| antelope |
| fox |
| beaver |
| coyote |
| horse |
| panther |
| lion |
| ??????? |

_____

_____

_____

_____

_____

_____

_____

_____

_____

_____

_____

_____

_____

See? We told you—all good things come *three* by *three!*

WRITING TECHNIQUE

# 10

A skillful use of <u>appositives</u> will help you to say more in fewer words. It's sort of like high octane gas: it enables you to get farther on less fuel. *Use* this technique regularly.

"BE

SINCERE ...

BE

BRIEF ...

BE

SEATED"

USE

PARALLEL

STRUCTURE

THE ELEVENTH STEP TO BETTER WRITING is to use **parallel structure**: parallel parts of a sentence should be similar in structure. With parallel structure, your sentences will be orderly and clear, will be rhythmical, will be easy to read and to remember.

> "I arrived in Hollywood without having *my nose fixed*, *my teeth capped*, or *my name changed*. That is very gratifying to me." (Barbra Streisand)
>
> "*Becoming number one* is easier than *remaining number one*." (Bill Bradley)
>
> "Love does not begin and end the way we ... think it does. *Love is a battle*; *love is a war*; *love is a growing up*." (James Baldwin)

Professional writers cherish **parallel structure**; professional speakers adore it; and *you* will applaud it—once you have learned to use it.

# 31

## PARALLEL STRUCTURE

# LEARN IT!

As the animals boarded Noah's Ark, they marched along in pairs. A giraffe accompanied a giraffe, an elephant an elephant, and an aardvark an aardvark.

Remember that image: it may help you to remember what **parallel structure** is.

For as the animals paired off, so grammatical structures within a sentence pair off.

An **infinitive** should march with an **infinitive**.

> She loved **to skate** and **to ski**.

A **gerund** should march with a **gerund**.

> **Skating** and **skiing** were his favorite activities.

An **active verb** should march with an **active verb**.

> She **cleaned** the spark plugs and **changed** the oil.

In short—the parallel parts of a sentence should be similar in structure.

---

**PARALLEL STRUCTURE**

**Verbs go with verbs,
Infinitives with
    infinitives,
Prepositional phrases
    with prepositional
    phrases,
            etc.**

---

1. Begin by completing the parallel structure in the following sentences. (Some clues are given in the first five.)

    a. I enjoy swimming, jogging, and _____.
       (Add a gerund: a verb ending in "-ing.")

    b. Mr. Jones was accused of theft, forgery, and _____ .
       (Add another crime, noun form.)

    c. To win the war, the general tried both clever maneuvers and _____. (What else might a general try? Use an adjective-noun combination to parallel "clever maneuvers.")

d. _____ and developing pictures are her two favorite hobbies. (Name another hobby. Use a gerund + object to parallel "developing pictures.")

e. He was loved by his friends and _____ _____. (Add a verb + a prepositional phrase to parallel "loved by his friends.")

f. Her stories are always imaginative, exciting, and _____.

g. To study for the exam or _____. that was the decision I had to make.

h. In English class I learned how to write and _____.

i. In this arcade game, players are mesmerized by the ringing of bells and _____.

j. A politician should be ambitious, hardworking, and _____.

**B. IDENTIFY PARALLEL STRUCTURE**

Remember—parallel structure may refer to whole sentences, to dependent clauses, to infinitives, even to single words. Study the following sentences carefully; underline the parallel parts.

EXAMPLE: "They have dressed as backpackers to keep an eye on the trails leading to the tops of the cliffs, and they have staged surprise raids." (David Schonauer)

1. "Since the dawn of history, men have been intrigued ... fascinated, even obsessed by precious stones." (Franklin Mint ad)
   (*Clue: look for parallel verbs.*)

2. "In every ... headland, in every curving beach, in every grain of sand, there is a story of the earth." (Rachel Carson)
   (*Clue: look for parallel prepositional phrases.*)

3. "Grecian urns and Roman busts sit among the rooftops; gilded cherubs toot their horns; alligators double as seats; a peacock spreads a vibrant tail." (Michael Demarest, describing the Wonderwall of the New Orleans 1984 World Fair)
   (*Clue: none—too obvious!*)

4. "If he wins, he can take the credit; but if he loses, he'll have to take the blame." (George Steinbrenner of Billy Martin, former New York Yankees manager)

   (*Clue: look for parallel dependent clauses.*)

5. "To love what you do and to feel that it matters—how could anything be more fun?" (Katharine Graham)

   (*Clue: look for parallel infinitives.*)

## C. THINK—WITH PARALLEL STRUCTURE

As you saw in the preceding exercises, parallel structure helps you to write more smoothly. But it can do more than that. It can actually help you to think and to organize your thinking. Suppose you are asked what someone should do to have strong, healthy teeth. You reply:

**To have strong, healthy teeth, you should ...**

- brush after every meal,
- use dental floss at least once a day, and
- drink plenty of milk.

Notice that every parallel part begins the same way: in this case, with a verb. You try it.

1. QUESTION: Why do students work at part-time jobs?

   ANSWER: Students work at part-time jobs

   to buy gas for their cars,

   to_____, and

   to_____.

2. QUESTION: List three factors that affect the success of a supermarket.

   ANSWER: A successful supermarket

   should provide shopping carts for the convenience of the customers,

   should_____, and

   should_____.

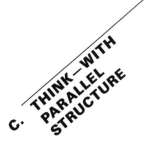

"The only way I can figure out what I really think about anything is to write about it."

Norman Mailer

176

**WEATHER HAZARDS**

hail
cyclone
drought
lightning
sleet
tornado
blizzard
flood

**3.** QUESTION: List three kinds of weather hazards common in the United States.

ANSWER: Common weather hazards in the U.S. include hurricanes, with sweeping rains and gale force winds,

_____, and

_____.

**4.** QUESTION: If a genie promised you three wishes, what three wishes would you make?

ANSWER: I would wish for

a million dollars,

_____, and

_____.

**5.** QUESTION: What three U.S. Presidents, living or dead, would you most like to meet? Why?

ANSWER: I would most like to meet

George Washington, because he was our first President and a fine general,

_____

_____, and

_____

_____.

Continue—completely on your own.

**6.** QUESTION: List three books you have enjoyed reading and explain *why* you enjoyed each.

ANSWER: _____

_____

_____

_____

**7.** QUESTION: Why do teenagers run away from home? Suggest three reasons.

ANSWER: _____

_____

_____

_____

_____

_____

**8.** QUESTION: Why are city streets sometimes dangerous?

ANSWER: _____

_____

_____

_____

_____

_____

**9.** QUESTION: Why are country roads sometimes dangerous?

ANSWER: _____

_____

_____

_____

_____

_____

**10.** QUESTION: What are some common causes of automobile accidents?

ANSWER: _____

_____

_____

_____

_____

_____

# 32

## PARALLEL STRUCTURE

## USE IT!

What are three important things to remember about making a speech?

> Well, one should be sincere.
> The speech should be brief.
> The speaker should sit down quickly.

Not very impressive, is it? But look what happens to the very same ideas when they are presented in terse parallel structure.

**Be sincere.**
**Be brief.**
**Be seated.**

Said James Roosevelt, son of Franklin Delano Roosevelt:

> My father gave me three hints on speech-making:
> "Be sincere . . . be brief . . . be seated."

Instead of rambling sentences, the Roosevelt version uses three short ones. Each of the three sentences begins with the imperative verb, "be."

Thanks to parallel structure, the recipe for a good speech is brief and effective.

Begin to use parallel structure by imitating the writing of others.

**A. LEARN BY IMITATING**

1.  "Be sincere . . . be brief . . . be seated." (Franklin D. Roosevelt)

    (CLUES: give a "recipe" for something you know how to do: for doing your homework; for making a sandwich; for creating an alibi when you're late. Then express it—in three brief parallel verbs or verb phrases. Example: a recipe for a toddler who wants a new toy—"*Beg, kick,* and *scream.* If all fails, *cry* piteously.")

    YOUR TURN:

    _____

    _____

**2.** *"Becoming* number one is easier than *remaining* number one." (Bill Bradley)

(CLUES:  write a similar sentence using *gerunds*: verbs ending in "-ing" and used as nouns. Example:  *"Winning* a contest is considerably harder than *entering* a contest.")

YOUR TURN:

_____

_____

**3.** "In every outthrust headland, in every curving beach, in every grain of sand, there is a story of the earth." (Rachel Carson)

(CLUES:  write a similar sentence using a series of prepositional phrases. Example: *"For days, for weeks, for months,* I studied algebra desperately.")

YOUR TURN:

_____

_____

**4.** "If you watch a game, it's fun. If you play it, it's recreation. If you work at it, it's golf." (Bob Hope)

(CLUES:  write a similarly structured series of sentences, each starting with a dependent clause. Example: *"When I order a banana split,* I am ecstatic. *When I dig into all that gooey wonder,* I am gloriously happy. *When I finish*—I am sick.")

YOUR TURN:

_____

_____

_____

**5.** "Love is a battle; love is a war; love is a growing up." (James Baldwin)

(CLUES:  write a series of three short sentences, all beginning with the same noun. Example: *"Fear* makes us tremble; *fear* makes us timid and afraid to act; *fear* makes us cowards.")

YOUR TURN:

_____

_____

_____

**180**

"Special" sentences, thanks to parallel structure, can add variety to your writing—and be fun at the same time.

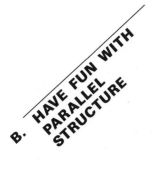

**B. HAVE FUN WITH PARALLEL STRUCTURE**

**1. For example . . .**

> *You* are muscle-bound; *I* am strong.

Get it? Two people with the same trait: in *you*, a vice; in *me*, a virtue! Another . . .

> *You* are pushy; *I* am aggressive.

YOUR TURN: Complete the following sentences.

**a.** *You* are reckless; *I* am _____.

**b.** *You* are timid; *I* am _____.

**c.** *You* are hungry for power; *I* am _____.

**2. For example . . .**

> Michael Jackson: *to hear* him is *to love* him.

A description and an evaluation—all in a few words, thanks to two parallel infinitives. Two more . . .

> Switzerland: *to visit* it is *to fall* under its enchantment.
> Beethoven: *to play* his music is *to harmonize* with angels.

YOUR TURN: Write a similar sentence of your own, using the name of any person or place, and a descriptive sentence with two parallel infinitives.

_____

_____

**3. For example . . .**

> *Many* are called, but *few* are chosen.

YOUR TURN: Use the "many . . . few" combination, or an "all . . . none" combination.

_____

_____

**4. For example . . .**

> "I'm not a stunt man . . . I'm not a daredevil . . . I'm an explorer." (Evel Knievel)

YOUR TURN: Follow the structure *exactly* in an original sentence of your own.

_____

_____

**5. For example . . .**

"Passing geometry is like climbing Mt. Everest: both seem impossible."

YOUR TURN: Follow the structure *exactly* in an original sentence of your own.

_____

_____

Now your work is getting tougher! First read the paragraph below written by a student.

**C. PLAY THE PROOFREADER**

> [1]Spending a day in an amusement park is fun—even if you're no longer a child. [2]I like the roller coaster. [3]The whip is fun, too. [4]And it's sort of fun to walk through the house of horrors. [5]Eating picnic-style appeals to me. [6]I really like those foot-long hot dogs—with everything. [7]Potato chips go well with it. [8]Sometimes I top it off with a big ice-cream cone. [9]I like chocolate.

Rather awkward, isn't it? Apparently this student never heard of parallel structure. Let's revise it a bit and see what happens.

First, we'll use parallel structure for sentences 2, 3, and 4. Like this . . .

ORIGINAL: I like the roller coaster. The whip is fun, too. And it's sort of fun to walk through the house of horrors.

REVISION: I like the roller coaster, the whip, and the house of horrors.

Next, we'll use parallel structure for sentences 5, 6, 7, 8, and 9. Like this . . .

ORIGINAL: Eating picnic-style appeals to me. I really like those foot-long hot dogs—with everything. Potato chips go well with it. Sometimes I top it off with a big ice-cream cone. I like chocolate.

REVISION: Eating picnic-style really appeals to me. I like eating those foot-long hot dogs (with everything), some potato chips on the side, and—to top it off—a big chocolate ice-cream cone!

That's better, isn't it?

But this student of ours doesn't know a great deal about writing at all. While we're revising, let's try a few more techniques.

The first revised sentence is now concise and clear—but it isn't very dramatic. We'll add a bit of detail.

> I like the ups-and-downs of the roller coaster, the sharp snap of the whip, and the eerieness of the house of horrors.

Come to think of it—the verb "like" is weak. Let's change it to "thrill to" and expand the parallel structure to include two more active verbs:

> I *thrill* to the ups-and-downs of the roller coaster, *gasp* at the sharp snap of the whip, and *shudder* at the eerieness of the house of horrors.

Now—let's look at the second revised sentence. We'll add a word or two, change "I like" to "Imagine devouring" (this forces reader participation), and toss in a couple of adjectives:

> And eating picnic-style appeals to me, too. Imagine devouring one of those foot-long hot dogs (with mustard, relish, and the works, of course!), some crispy potato chips, and—to top it off—a gigantic chocolate fudge ice-cream cone!

Finally, let's put it all together. Here's the revised paragraph.

> Spending a day in an amusement park is fun—even if your're no longer a kid. I thrill to the ups-and-downs of the roller coaster, gasp at the sharp snap of the whip, and shudder at the eerieness of the house of horrors. And eating picnic-style appeals to me, too. Imagine devouring one of those foot-long hot dogs (with mustard, relish, and the works, of course!), some crispy potato chips, and—to top it off—a gigantic chocolate fudge ice-cream cone!

The new paragraph is only one line longer than the original, but it says much more, is easier to read and to understand, and is far more dramatic.

Now it's your turn. We promised you a tough assignment, and here it is. Read the student-written paragraph below.

> Spending a day in an electronic-game arcade is fun. The game "Asteroids" is my favorite. I like "PacMan" too. "Moon Patrol" is also fun. There are always lots of flashing lights. Loud noises fill the place. Shrieks from the players can be heard. It's kind of exciting. It makes me feel alive. I never find that time goes slowly when I'm in a games arcade.

It's all yours! Revise it.

☐ Use parallel structure.

☐ Use sentence variety.

☐ Add specific action verbs.

☐ Add appropriate adjectives.

☐ Change word order—sentence types— sentence structure—anything you like . . .

. . . so long as you end with a fast-moving description of a day in a games arcade.

That's your challenge! Go to it.

_____

_____

_____

_____

_____

_____

_____

_____

_____

_____

_____

_____

_____

_____

"To make you feel; to make you hear; to make you touch; to make you see— that is my aim."

**Joseph Conrad**

# 33

## PARALLEL STRUCTURE

## USE IT IN **YOUR** WRITING!

---

**A.** 1. **Parallel structure** is helpful when you want to describe something in an amusing or touching way.

> What is a boy's pocket? A boy's pocket is the home of snails and frogs and other delectable creatures. A boy's pocket is a resting place for_____
> _____. A boy's pocket is a treasure chest of_____
> _____.

Complete the above paragraph, developing sentences three and four, following sentence two as a guide. Be as imaginative as you can—and search for exactly the right nouns and adjectives.

2. Next, write a paragraph of your own, following the structure of the paragraph in exercise 1. Begin with a rhetorical question: "What is a (an)_____?" (Fill the blank with any ordinary thing you would like to write about: a hall closet; a kitchen drawer; a purse; a suitcase; a small end table.) And—of course—use parallel structure in sentences 2,3, and 4.

**RHETORICAL QUESTION:**

**A question you ask, intending to answer it yourself.**

_____

_____

_____

_____

_____

_____

_____

_____

_____

**185**

**B.** **1.** **Parallel structure** is useful when you want to describe a process.

PARALLEL STRUCTURE
helps you to
THINK!

> We will do whatever is necessary to win this election. We will create jazzy slogans and give away balloons and whistles. We will_____
>
> _____.
>
> We will_____
>
> _____. And we *will* win!

Complete the above paragraph, developing sentences 3 and 4, using sentence 2 as a guide. Again—be imaginative; be dramatic; be concise.

**2.** Now write a paragraph of your own, following the structure of the paragraph above. Begin with one of the simple statements below (or a similar one).

> We will do whatever is necessary to win this _____ game.
>
> We will do whatever is necessary to save our country.
>
> We will do whatever is necessary to make this garage sale a success.
>
> I will do anything to pass this course.
>
> I will do anything to earn money.

Write sentences 2, 3, and 4, explaining exactly *what* you will do to achieve your goal—and write them using parallel structure.

_____

_____

_____

_____

_____

_____

_____

**C.** Finally, think back over your life. Find a period that was memorable—perhaps wonderful, perhaps horrible. Some possibilities: two weeks when you and your family toured the country; one week which you spent in the hospital having an operation; a month when you were at summer camp. Probe your memory. Then write your title below.

_____of My Life
(Mention time period—example, "Two Weeks.")

**1.** Next, think about this period in your life and divide your memories into three categories.

EXAMPLE:  "One Week of My Life" (in the hospital)

CATEGORY 1:  Things I Did to Pass the Time
2:  Hospital Routine Drives Patients Crazy
3:  How I Felt About Visitors

Decide what *your* three categories will be and write them on the first line of each cluster below.

1. _____

   a. _____

   b. _____

   c. _____

2. _____

   a. _____

   b. _____

   c. _____

3. _____

   a. _____

   b. _____

   c. _____

**2.** Now complete each cluster above. For example, for a cluster about "Things I did to pass the time in the hospital," you might note: jigsaw puzzles—talking to the patient in the next bed—reading magazines. Select from your memory the three most interesting items for each cluster and write them in the spaces above.

3. Write an introductory paragraph. Keep your title in mind *and* the kinds of memories you are going to be talking about. Make this paragraph a true introduction, but make it interesting. You may wish to start with a rhetorical question, with a quotation, or with a brief anecdote.

_____

_____

_____

_____

_____

4. Write a paragraph that follows logically from paragraph 1 and that is about category #1. You should find parallel structure a useful technique here.

_____

_____

_____

_____

_____

5. Write a paragraph that is about category #2.

_____

_____

_____

_____

_____

6. Write a paragraph that is about category #3.

_____

_____

_____

_____

_____

7. Write a concluding paragraph—one that sums up what you said and that is amusing or provocative. Keep it brief—about two sentences.

_____

_____

_____

8. Now revise exercises 3 through 7. Be sure your sentence structure is varied; that you have used strong exact words; that you have used some parallel structure. Make any corrections necessary.

9. Copy the complete essay (title + introductory paragraph + three paragraphs + concluding paragraph) below.

_____

_____

_____

_____

_____

_____

_____

_____

_____

_____

_____

_____

_____

_____

_____

_____

_____

_____

_____

_____

_____

_____

> "True ease in writing comes from art, not chance,
> As those move easiest who have learn'd to dance."
>
> Alexander Pope

[continued]

## WRITING TECHNIQUE

# 11 ━━━━━━━━━━━━

**Parallel structure is a little like a magical polish: rub a bit on and your writing will absolutely shine! It's a good technique; use it.**

# KEYWORD:

## PIGS

## USE

## VERBALS

THE TWELFTH STEP TO BETTER WRITING is to use **verbals:** *participles* (P), *infinitives* (I), and *gerunds* (G). Notice that the first letters of the three words spell PIG. Let that be your keyword!

---

SHEILA GRAHAM: ''Hollywood ... a world of dwarfs *casting* long shadows.'' (**participle**)

PETER FALK: ''It took me nine years *to get* married, ten *to become* an actor.'' (**infinitives**)

SHIRLEY BOOTH: ''*Acting* is a way to overcome your own inhibitions and shyness.'' (**gerund**)

---

**Verbals** lend speed and excitement to your writing. Learn them—and use them.

# 34

## VERBALS

## LEARN THEM!

A <u>performing</u> pig is able <u>to impress</u> an audience by <u>galloping</u> to country music.

Memorize the keyword, **Pig,** and the sentence above and you will have no trouble remembering the three kinds of verbals and what they are! To wit ...

VERBAL    EXAMPLE

*Participle*—*Performing*

*Infinitive*—to *Impress*

*Gerund*  — *Galloping*

Now—isn't that easy? Of course, there's a bit more to know about these three verbals ...

**A. PARTICIPLE PANORAMA**

A **participle** is a verb to which "-ing" or "-ed" (usually) has been added and which is used as an *adjective*.

A <u>whistling</u> teakettle is a comfort on a winter night.

An <u>uninterrupted</u> conversation is seldom possible.

Our conversation was <u>interrupted</u>.

<u>Grinning</u>, Jenny accepted the award.

**1.** In the following sentences, underline the participle and draw an arrow to the noun it modifies.

  **a.** A dancing pig dressed in pants and ribbons amused King

     Louis XI in the late 15th century.

b. Some exhausted marathoners quit after eighteen miles.

c. Hog-calling contests are popular at county fairs all over America.

d. The Wright brothers invented a flying machine.

e. Sal is worried about his grades.

When a participle is combined with other related words, the result is a **participial phrase.** Like a participle, a participial phrase is used as an *adjective*. Remember: an adjective modifies a noun.

My brother, troubled by the latest news, enlisted in the army.

A teakettle, whistling merrily, gave comfort on a winter night.

The officer approached the suspect hiding in the doorway.

2. In the following sentences, underline the participial phrase and draw an arrow to the noun or pronoun it modifies.

a. The largest hog in the world is the Borean Pig measuring six feet in length.

b. In the early 1900s, twenty-one piglets, nicknamed "Fred's Pigs," played on a seesaw, climbed a ladder, and balanced balls on their snouts.

c. Biting more savagely than a tiger, the wild boar is a dangerous enemy.

**d.** Frightened by the huge waves, Allie refused to enter the water.

**e.** Eddie, panting for air, rounded third base and headed for home.

**3.** Now create a few participial phrases of your own. We'll give you a verb; you add the indicated ending (correctly spelled, of course). Add a noun and other related words to form a participial phrase. Then use the phrase in a sentence as an *adjective* (modifying a *noun*).

**a.** *run*(-ing)_____

_____

_____

**b.** *sob*(-ing)_____

_____

_____

**c.** *shatter*(-ed)_____

_____

_____

**d.** *terrify*(-ed)_____

_____

_____

**e.** *beat*(-en)_____

_____

_____

---

**PARTICIPLES**

**Present participles end in** *-ing.*
   *jumping* **frog**
   *glittering* **diamonds**

**Past participles usually end in** *-ed,* **but some in** *-en* **or** *-t.*
   *trained* **lions**
   *broken* **promises**
   *burnt* **toast**

---

"Infrangible" means—cannot be broken, cannot be separated into parts. Infinitives cannot—or should not—be broken.

INCORRECT: *to* quickly *write*      CORRECT: *to write* quickly
INCORRECT: *to* slowly *wander*      CORRECT: *to wander* slowly

An infinitive = *to* + a verb: *to leap, to dance, to write, to fight*. Don't confuse infinitives with prepositional phrases. "To the store" is a prepositional phrase; so is "to Russia." Remember: To form an infinitive, the word that follows "to" *must* be a verb.

An infinitive may be used as a *noun, adjective,* or *adverb*.

To eat is a necessity.
    (used as a noun, subject of the verb "is")

She has a desire to write.
    (used as an adjective, modifying the noun "desire")

We stopped to shop.
    (used as an adverb, modifying the verb "stopped")

1.  In the following sentences, identify the infinitive by underlining it. (*Beware:* a few "to + a noun" prepositional phrases have been included.)

    a.  After going to the store, Lou had time to play.

    b.  To sing on stage is her one desire.

    c.  She went to bed to sleep.

    d.  After watching *Peter Pan*, Merrilee tried to fly.

    e.  Although we have never won before, today we hope to win.

---

**Each proverb is lacking an infinitive. Can you provide them?**

Early to bed and early _____ _____,
Makes a man healthy, wealthy and wise.

It takes two _____ _____ a bargain.

He that fights and runs away,
May live _____ _____ another day.

_____ _____ is human, _____ _____ divine.

---

When an infinitive is combined with other related words, the result is an **infinitive phrase.** Like the infinitive, the infinitive phrase is used as a *noun*, an *adjective*, or an *adverb*.

> To be late to school every day is a no-no.
> (used as a noun, the subject of the verb "is")

> Her plan to lengthen the school year was unpopular.
> (used as an adjective modifying the noun "plan")

> I was too happy to think about the time.
> (used as an adverb modifying the adjective "happy")

**2.** In the following sentences, underline the infinitive phrases. (There may be more than one in a sentence.)

    **a.** Darrell hiked to the ice-cream parlor to relax with a chocolate sundae.

    **b.** A pet pig can easily be taught to fetch a newspaper, to pull a cart, or to play the piano.

    **c.** In 1886, someone dared Steve Brodie to jump off the Brooklyn Bridge.

    **d.** To everyone's amazement, Brodie did so and lived to talk about it.

    **e.** Years later, when someone dared him to try it again, Brodie said (ungrammatically): "I done it oncet."

**3.** Now create a few infinitive phrases of your own. We'll give you a verb; you place a "to" before it. Add related words to the infinitive and form an infinitive phrase. Then use the phrase in a sentence.

    **a.** *grin*_____

    _____

    **b.** *report*_____

    _____

    **c.** *tame*_____

    _____

    **d.** *haunt*_____

    _____

    **e.** *break*_____

    _____

**Caution: The word *to* is the "sign of the infinitive." To avoid confusing an infinitive with the preposition *to*, check the word that follows *to*. If it is a verb, then the expression is an *infinitive.***

A **gerund** is a verb to which "-ing" has been added and which is used as a *noun*. A gerund may be the subject of a verb or the object of a verb or of a preposition.

> One popular art form is whistling.
> (used as a predicate noun after the verb "is")

> She enjoys jogging.
> (used as object of the verb "enjoys")

> He was arrested for speeding.
> (used as object of the preposition "for")

**1.** In the following sentences, underline the gerunds.

   **a.** Talking is his favorite pastime.

   **b.** His favorite hobby is skiing.

   **c.** She has a deep interest in dancing.

   **d.** José bought new equipment suitable for hiking.

   **e.** Thinking should precede writing.

When a gerund is combined with other related words, the result is a **gerund phrase**. Remember: a gerund or a gerund phrase is always used as a *noun*.

> Wishing for the moon is a waste of time.
> (used as subject of the verb "is")

> I appreciate your helping me with the dishes.
> (used as direct object of the verb "appreciate")

> The man was arrested for driving while intoxicated.
> (used as object of the preposition "for")

**2.** In the following sentences, underline the gerund phrases.

   **a.** President William Howard Taft enjoyed golfing with his friends even though he weighed over 330 pounds.

   **b.** By using motorized roller skates, you can travel 220 miles on one gallon of gas.

   **c.** Learning to fly is difficult for a duckling.

**d.** Often the duckling can't quite take off, even after flapping its wings furiously. Thus the word "flapper" came into existence.

**e.** Acting like an adult doesn't make one an adult, young girls learned. It just makes them "flappers."

**3.** Now create a few gerund phrases of your own. We'll give you a verb; you add "-ing." Then add related words to the gerund to form a gerund phrase. Use the phrase in a sentence as a *noun*.

**a.** *swim* _____

_____

**b.** *swing* _____

_____

**c.** *try* _____

_____

**d.** *polish* _____

_____

**e.** *comb* _____

_____

> **Caution: A gerund may be confused with a present participle because both verbals end in -*ing*. Remember: a gerund is used as a noun, a participle as an adjective.**

```
Remember:   P—participle
            I—infinitive
            G—gerund
```

# 35

## VERBALS

## USE THEM!

Verbals are useful, but they're also tricky. Sometimes, if you're not careful, verbals can turn you into a comic when you're trying hard *not* to be one!

One problem with verbal phrases is that writers sometimes place them incorrectly in the sentence. For example:

A. DANGLING AND MISPLACED VERBAL PHRASES

MISPLACED: Looking like a monster with red, glittering eyes,

I stared at the enormous new robot.

Because the participial phrase (underlined) is misplaced, the sentence suggests that "I" look like a monster with red, glittering eyes—surely not the writer's intention! The phrase should be placed near the noun or pronoun it modifies *or* should be changed to a clause. Like this...

CLEAR: I stared at the enormous new robot [looking like a monster with red, glittering eyes].

OR:

CLEAR: I stared at the enormous new robot [which looked

like a monster with red, glittering eyes].

Another problem with verbal phrases is that writers sometimes let them "dangle"—that is, place them in a sentence without providing a suitable word to modify.

DANGLING: By turning the VOLUME dial to the right, the screen will light up.

The nearest word for the verbal phrase to modify is "screen"—but surely a screen can't turn a dial! The sentence must be rewritten to be clear. Add a noun or pronoun for the phrase to modify *or* change the phrase to a clause.

CLEAR: By turning the VOLUME dial to the right, a viewer will light up the screen.

OR:

CLEAR: If you turn the VOLUME dial to the right, the screen will light up.

Get it? Correct the following sentences by changing the position of the verbal phrase, by changing a verbal phrase to a clause, or by adding a noun or pronoun for the phrase to modify. (Which you decide to do depends on the sentence and common sense.)

1. Acting as a sort of sanitation department, the streets in the 16th century were kept clear of waste food by the pigs.

   _____

   _____

   _____

2. To produce a litter of eight to ten healthy piglets twice a year, a farmer needs only a well-fed sow.

   _____

   _____

   _____

3. After going to the institute for two years, jobs are guaranteed for all graduates.

   _____

   _____

   _____

4. Playing inside the cage, we watched the antics of the monkeys.

   _____

   _____

   _____

5. A four-line jingle about pigs must be written to win the contest.

   _____

   _____

   _____

6. Maps should be studied and guide books carefully checked before visiting Washington, D.C.

   _____

   _____

   _____

**7.** Standing on the street corner, a truck smashed me to the ground.

_____

_____

**8.** We reveled in the beauty and serenity of Central Park riding in a hansom cab.

_____

_____

**9.** After enduring sleet, hailstones, and hurricane winds, the haystack was a welcome refuge.

_____

_____

**10.** To be eligible for the first prize, three box tops must be submitted with the entry.

_____

_____

_____

**B. COMBINING SENTENCES**

In each of the following clusters, there are two short choppy sentences. Combine them into one good sentence by using a **verbal**.

**1.** A female pig or hog is called a _sow_. Sow is pronounced to rhyme with _cow_.

_____

_____

_____

**2.** In Cincinnati in 1863, over 600,000 hogs were slaughtered. At that time people called Cincinnati "Porkopolis."

_____

_____

_____

**3.** Pigs often wallow in mud. It cools them off.

_____

_____

_____

**4.** In London, in 1789, the "Learned Pig" wrote words. It picked up letters written on cards and arranged them.

_____

_____

_____

_____

**5.** Charles Braverman of Chicago collects pig memorabilia. He owns a $2,000 brass pig dinner bell and a $2,400 pig ashtray.

_____

_____

_____

_____

**6.** Salt pork was smuggled past British sentries at night in 1776. The salt pork provided food for Washington's troops at Valley Forge.

_____

_____

_____

_____

**7.** Most pigs don't go to school. Therefore it is difficult to find a trained pig.

_____

_____

_____

_____

The following story about **pigs** appeared on your editorial desk. Read it.

¹Pigs have been around for a long time. ²In millions of years, they have changed little. ³They still have fourteen ribs. ⁴They still have 44 teeth. ⁵They still have cloven hooves. ⁶They are round and short-legged. ⁷Their skin is thick. ⁸It is covered with short, coarse bristles. ⁹Pigs have long snouts. ¹⁰They have small curly tails. ¹¹They carry their heads low. ¹²They eat and drink close to the ground. ¹³They breathe close to the ground, too. ¹⁴Some are white with black on their faces and legs. ¹⁵Some are red. ¹⁶Some have white spots on a black background. ¹⁷A few are black and have a white belt around the body. ¹⁸Centuries ago, pigs were used as scavengers. ¹⁹They kept the streets clean. ²⁰Today they provide food. ²¹Pork comes from pigs and is a popular food. ²²From pigs come bacon and sausages. ²³Pigs eat everything. ²⁴They eat potatoes and artichokes. ²⁵Snakes and birds they eat, too. ²⁶They even eat earthworms and insects and nuts. ²⁷A New England farmer once said, ''Dogs look up to you, cats look down on you, and pigs think you're their equal.'' ²⁸Pigs are fascinating animals.

After reading it, you decide to use the story, but you also decide it needs a total rewriting. Do it now, after reading the suggestions below.

**a.** Start with a strong sentence, possibly #27.

**b.** Combine...

| | |
|---|---|
| 1 and 2 | 14 and 15 |
| 3, 4, and 5 | 16 and 17 |
| 6, 7, and 8 | 18 and 19 |
| 9 and 10 | 20, 21, and 22 |
| 11, 12, and 13 | 23, 24, and 25 |

**c.** The above are only suggestions. You should use your own judgment as you rewrite, but do remember to use, when needed...

participles, infinitives, and gerunds

parallel structure

appositives

prepositional phrases

subordinate clauses

... and any other writing techniques that will be helpful. This is a sort of proofreading marathon—so do your best!

# 36

## VERBALS

## USE THEM IN YOUR WRITING!

**A.** **1.** Below is a topic sentence and the beginning of a second sentence. Your job is to write a paragraph developing the topic sentence. Do it—by inserting a series of infinitives. Add at least two sentences. You will find all the information you need in Chapters 34 and 35.

Pigs can be taught to do almost anything! They

can be taught _____

_____

_____

_____

_____

**2.**           *Gerbils jump a lot, and they burrow into*
          *the ground to make their homes.*

With this information plus some commonsense, you should be able to complete the following paragraph by inserting *two* participles, *two* infinitives, and *two* gerunds. We challenge you!

Gerbils are small _____

desert rodents. By _____ deep

into the ground, they make themselves cool, comfort-

able homes. _____ grass-lined chambers,

these homes provide moisture as well as safety from

predators. _____ small forelegs and

long hind legs enable gerbils _____

rapidly. It is normal for gerbils _____

to a dozen young at a time.

**B.** Pigs (as you have seen) are popular! Everyone knows Miss Piggy, and some of you may remember Arnold, the clever pig who starred in the TV show, "Green Acres." You are being asked to use your imagination for this assignment.

**1.** Dream up a pig that can do something unusual; then give this pig an unusual or catchy name. _____

**2.** Create a weekly TV show in which this pig will star. Give the show an appealing title. _____

**3.** Write two paragraphs.

In the first paragraph, describe the pig: what it would wear, how it would act, and so forth. Consider using a generalization-to-details organization. (See page 13.)

In the second paragraph, describe the TV show: the kinds of incidents that would be used, the kinds of humor that would result. Consider using a categorical organization. (See pages 113–114.)

As you write, remember to call upon all the various writing techniques you have been learning, especially verbals.

## PIG LEXICON

**swine**—whole family including pigs, boars, etc.

**pig**—young swine

**boar**—male swine

**sow**—adult female swine

**hog**—swine weighing more than 120 pounds

**piglet**—small young hog

**porker**—young pig fattened for table use

**piggery**—place where swine are kept

**pigsty**—pen housing swine

**snout**—long, projecting nose common to swine

**porcine**—piglike

**porkpie**—hat with a flat top and turned up brim

_____

_____

_____

_____

_____

_____

_____

_____

_____

_____

_____

_____

_____

_____

_____

_____

_____

**Is your closet a PIGSTY?**

**C.** As your third assignment, describe a **pigsty.** You've never seen one, you say? Of course you have! Just consider these possible topics...

  (a) your bedroom

  (b) a cabinet that has become a family catch-all

  (c) a closet that must be opened carefully if you don't wish to be hit on the head

  (d) "the pigsty of your mind" (Example: right now you should be concentrating solely on this assignment, but you probably have a dozen other things cluttering up your mind: that you're too hot (or too cold); that you hope it doesn't rain; that the big game is tomorrow; that your ankle itches; that... You see?)

  (e) or—a real pigsty

*Step 1:* Select the pigsty that you will describe. Remember the rule: choose something you know about. If your bedroom is always neat, *don't* choose "a." If your mind tends to wander and to jump from topic to topic, *do* choose "d." Choose now...

_____

*Step 2:* Think about *your* pigsty. Make notes. Ask yourself questions like these ...

Can you recall any sharp or amusing image?

(Example: a disassembled bicycle in the middle of your bedroom)

Can you recall an interesting anecdote?

(Example: you spent an hour looking for your baseball bat, then opened the hall closet and had it fall on your head.)

Can you recall some memorable words spoken by a parent, a sibling (sister or brother), or a friend?

(Example: "Your bedroom looks like a dinosaur's playground!")

  After asking (and answering) questions like these, make some relevant notes below.

_____
_____
_____
_____
_____
_____
_____

| PIGSTY WORDS | |
|---|---|
| **Nouns** | |
| jungle | maze |
| wilderness | litter |
| muddle | chaos |
| **Verbs** | |
| rumple | botch |
| bungle | fester |
| reek | wallow |
| **Adjectives** | |
| grimy | abominable |
| dirty | mouldy |
| slimy | rusty |
| squalid | rotten |
| dusty | bedraggled |
| topsy-turvy | disorderly |
| messy | chaotic |

*Step 3:* Organize your notes. Consider a **spatial** organization (see page 75) if you are working with topic ''a,'' ''b,'' ''c,'' or ''e.'' Consider a **categorical** organization (see pages 113–114) if you are dealing with topic ''d.'' On scrap paper, outline your possible organization.

*Step 4:* Now, still working on scrap paper, write a description of *your* pigsty. (Remember to use **verbals** and other writing techniques.) Make your description as clear and amusing as you can.

*Step 5:* Revise your description, again remembering the various writing techniques you have been practicing.

*Step 6:* Copy the final draft below.

_____

_____

_____

_____

_____

_____

_____

_____

_____

_____

_____

_____

_____

_____

_____

_____

_____

_____

_____

## WRITING TECHNIQUE 12

For agile action—for cutting clarity—for sentence smoothness—use verbals. This technique, like the eleven that precede it, will improve your writing *and* your thinking.

# COMBINATIONS
# GALORE!

# USE
# SENTENCE
# COMBINING

THE THIRTEENTH STEP TO BETTER WRITING is to use **sentence combining**: a technique that turns several short, choppy sentences into one smooth, effective one.

> WHY SAY ... ?
> *There was a full moon. The full moon gave light. Two boys sneaked into a graveyard. They were hoping to catch a glimpse of a ghost. The ghost they were hoping to see was the Galloping Ghost.*
>
> WHY NOT SAY ... ?
> *In the light of the full moon, two boys sneaked into a graveyard, hoping to catch a glimpse of the Galloping Ghost.*

Without **sentence combining**, your writing will putter along like an old car; with sentence combining, it will race like a new Jaguar, carrying your readers with you.

So simple a technique to yield so complex a reward. Use it!

# 37

## COMBINING SENTENCES
## NURSERY LEVEL

Too many short, choppy sentences? Combine them!

Of course, that's just what you have been doing—using appositives, verbals, prepositional phrases, and other writing techniques. But so far, you have been doing it by formula: combining sentences according to specific instructions. Now you may give your imagination free rein! Sentences, you will find, can be combined in many ways.

Consider these two sentences:

---

The dog skittered on its hind legs. It danced to the music of the Scottish bagpipes.

---

*We can say...*

Dancing to the music of the Scottish bagpipes, the dog skittered on its hind legs.

*OR...*

The dog skittered on its hind legs as it danced to the music of the Scottish bagpipes.

*OR...*

Skittering on its hind legs, the dog danced to the music of the Scottish bagpipes.

*OR (giving the sentences a new twist)...*

The music of the Scottish bagpipes stirred the dog to skitter on its hind legs.

*OR...*

The dog, skittering on its hind legs, danced to the music of the Scottish bagpipes.

*OR...*

The dog, dancing to the music of the Scottish bagpipes, skittered on its hind legs.

*OR...*

On its hind legs, the dog skittered, dancing to the music of the Scottish bagpipes.

*OR...*

To the music of the Scottish bagpipes, the dog danced, skittering on its hind legs.

*OR...*

One could continue, practically forever!

Ready for your own "tour de force"? (See page 145.)

**A.** Start with these two sentences.

**The cow jumped over the moon. The little dog laughed.**

See how many ways you can combine the two sentences. You should easily be able to find six combinations; but can you find twelve?

_____

_____

_____

_____

_____

_____

_____

_____

_____

_____

---

According to legend, Elizabeth Goose often lulled her grandchildren to sleep with catchy little songs. Thomas Fleet, her son-in-law and a Boston printer, was "driven distracted" by the songs and swore to get revenge by printing the melodies for all the world to hear. He did—in 1719—and that was the first "Songs for the Nursery" by Mother Goose.

**B.** Another "tour de force":

> Little Tommy Tucker sang for his supper. He sang for brown bread and butter.

Can you combine these two sentences in *five* ways? Try!

_____

_____

_____

_____

_____

_____

_____

_____

Many of the Mother Goose rhymes are much older than Elizabeth Goose . . . and many refer to real people.

"Jack Sprat could eat no fat," for example, appeared in print in 1639 and was used to make fun of Archdeacon Pratt and his wife Joan.

"Little Tommy Tucker" may refer to a particular troubadour. The troubadours were performers who entertained in inns and taverns in exchange for supper.

Another . . .

> Little Bo Peep has lost her sheep. She doesn't know where to find them.

Combine these two sentences in *five* ways.

_____

_____

_____

_____

_____

_____

_____

_____

_____

Bo Peep probably refers to an old nursery game in which the mother covers the baby's face for a moment, then removes the covering and cries "Bo-peep!" Today a mother covers her face with her hands, removes them, and cries—"Peek-a-boo!"

**D.** One more...

**Jack and Jill went up the hill. They went to fetch a pail of water.**

Again, try to combine these two sentences in *five* ways.

_____

_____

_____

_____

_____

_____

_____

_____

_____

Nursery rhymes aren't always charming. Of the 200 believed to belong to "Mother Goose," about 100 are tainted with violence, including murder, kidnapping, and whippings.

# 38

## COMBINING SENTENCES

## JUNIOR LEVEL

You hurdled Level I. You're ready for Level II! Below is a barrage of sentence clusters--just crying to be combined. Your assignment: combine the sentences in each cluster into one smooth, well-constructed sentence using any technique you like.

1. The first Martian appeared on March 1st. March 1st was a Sunday. Everybody was in church.

   _____

   _____

2. Three tramps invaded our tiny town. The dogs all began barking madly.

   _____

   _____

3. It was cold and dark. Dana slipped out of the house at midnight.

   _____

   _____

4. Max liked apples. He especially liked Mackintosh apples. He liked oranges that were big and juicy. He liked cherries.

   _____

   _____

   _____

5. Joyce-Ann swims. She swims in the Community Pool. The Community Pool is Olympic-size. She swims every day.

   _____

   _____

   _____

**6.** Two billion dollars is spent every year in this country on dog food. There are about forty million dogs in the U.S.

_____

_____

**7.** A slanted line sometimes divides dates and choices (4/4/84; he/she). This slanted line is called a virgule.

_____

_____

_____

**8.** Every year Americans devour about 200,000 tons of popcorn. Much of it is consumed in movie theaters.

_____

_____

**9.** Paul Bunyan had a blue ox. The blue ox was called Babe. It measured 42 axe handles and a plug of chewing tobacco between its horns.

_____

_____

_____

**10.** This happened in France in the 15th century. Nobles enjoyed batting a cloth ball back and forth. They often shouted, "Tenez" which means "Take it." So the game of _tennis_ was born. (Hint: start with "Tennis was born in France . . .")

_____

_____

_____

_____

_____

**DID YOU KNOW . . .**

That a good tennis ball contains 14 pounds of air? That 50% of all tennis players over 35 suffer from tennis elbow? That tennis was brought to this country in 1874 by Mary Ewing Outerbridge?

# 39

## COMBINING SENTENCES
## SENIOR LEVEL

Did you know that...

...an alligator can run faster than a human being--up to 150 feet?

...it takes fifteen months to train a bandleader at the Pentagon's School of Music, but only thirteen months to train a jet pilot?

...Eskimos use refrigerators to keep food *from* freezing?

If you enjoy odd information of this type, you will find Isaac Asimov's *Book of Facts* a delight. Browse through it some time. Meanwhile, sample some more of Asimov's treasure trove as you work on these exercises.

Below are ten brief paragraphs—*not* as Asimov wrote them. Rewrite each, using the directions given. The directions grow less specific as you proceed. When you have finished, you will feel like a magician—for you will have made dead writing come alive!

1.  ¹Gene Tunney was a heavyweight boxing champion. ²He also lectured on Shakespeare at Yale University. (Combine into one sentence.)

    Combine the two sentences, using an appositive.

    *Your rewrite*:_____

    _____

    _____

2.  ¹Sergei Prokofiev was a Russian composer. ²He composed an opera. ³This opera was called "The Giant." ⁴He was then seven years old. ⁵The opera used only the white keys on the piano. (Combine into two sentences.)

    **a.** Combine 1 and 2, using an appositive.

    **b.** Combine 1-2 revised, with 4, turning 4 into a dependent clause.

    **c.** Combine 3 and 5, using an appositive.

*Your rewrite*: _____

_____

_____

3. ¹Whitcomb L. Judson was a Chicago inventor. ²In 1891, he took out a patent for the zipper. ³He meant it to replace buttons on shoes. ⁴He called it the "Clasp Locker and Unlocker for Shoes." (Combine into two sentences.)

   a. Combine 1 and 2, using an appositive.

   b. Change the position of the prepositional phrase, "In 1891," placing it at the beginning or end of the revised sentence.

   c. Combine 3 and 4 by turning 3 into a participial phrase beginning with "Meaning..."

*Your rewrite*: _____

_____

_____

4. ¹Richard Blechynden, an Englishman, sold tea at the St. Louis World's Fair. ²That was in 1904. ³One day it was intolerably hot. ⁴Nobody wanted hot tea. ⁵Blechynden tried serving it cold. ⁶The result? ⁷Iced tea! (Combine into five sentences.)

   a. Combine sentences 1 and 2.

   b. Combine sentences 3 and 4 into a simple sentence.

   c. Keep sentences 5, 6, and 7.

*Your rewrite*: _____

_____

_____

_____

5. ¹St. Patrick was actually British. ²He saw Ireland for the first time when he was kidnapped by some Irishmen. ³He escaped. ⁴He became a priest. ⁵He then became a bishop. ⁶Finally, he became a missionary. ⁷He went back to Ireland. ⁸He was highly successful in his missionary work there. ⁹He became the patron saint of Ireland. (Combine into five sentences.)

**a.** Keep sentences 1 and 2.

**b.** Turn sentence 3 into a dependent clause beginning with "After..."

**c.** Combine sentence 3 revised with sentences 4, 5, and 6, using parallel structure.

**d.** Combine sentences 7 and 8 into a complex sentence.

**e.** Keep sentence 9.

*Your rewrite:* _____

_____

_____

_____

_____

**6.** [1]Rudyard Kipling lived in Brattleboro, Vermont, for five years. [2]Kipling liked outdoor exercise even in winter. [3]In Vermont, it snows frequently. [4]Kipling invented snow golf. [5]He painted golf balls red. [6]Then he could locate them in the snow. [7]Kipling was the author of *The Jungle Books* and *Kim*. (Combine into four sentences.)

**a.** Combine sentences 1 and 7.

**b.** Combine sentences 2 and 3 into a compound sentence.

**c.** Combine sentence 3 (revised) with sentence 4.

**d.** Combine sentences 5 and 6.

*Your rewrite:* _____

_____

_____

_____

_____

How much is a **MILLION?**

Imagine a lot of people six feet tall. A million of them, lying down head to toe, would stretch from New York City to Des Moines, Iowa!

**7.** [1]In 1845 the population of Ireland was 8¼ million. [2]In 1848 Ireland was struck by a devastating potato famine. [3]By 1851 the population was down to 6½ million. [4]About one million had died. [5]About one million had emigrated. (Combine into three sentences.)

**a.** Keep sentence 1.

**b.** Combine sentences 2 and 3.

**c.** Combine sentences 4 and 5.

*Your rewrite:*_____

_____

_____

_____

_____

8. [1]James Barry joined the medical corps of the army of Queen Victoria. [2]He served as a surgeon for forty years. [3]He eventually was promoted to inspector-general of hospitals. [4]In 1865, he died. [5]After his death, it was discovered that ''he'' was a ''she.'' [6]Barry was a woman who had successfully masqueraded as a man for over forty years! (Combine into four sentences.)

**a.** Keep sentence 1.

**b.** Combine sentences 2 and 3.

**c.** Keep sentence 4.

**d.** Combine sentences 5 and 6.

*Your rewrite:*_____

_____

_____

_____

_____

_____

9. [1]Four friends were vacationing in Switzerland. [2]They agreed that each would write a ghost story. [3]The poets, Shelley and Byron, never finished theirs. [4]Neither did Dr. John Polidori. [5]But Mary Wollstonecraft Godwin did. [6]She was eighteen. [7]She was the wife of Percy Shelley. [8]That ghost story was published two years later, in 1818. [9]The story was called *Frankenstein*. (Combine into five sentences.)

**a.** Combine sentences 1 and 2.

**b.** Combine sentences 3 and 4.

**c.** Keep sentence 5.

**d.** Combine sentences 6 and 7.

**e.** Combine sentences 8 and 9.

*Your rewrite:*_____

_____

_____

_____

_____

_____

_____

**10.** [1]The Brothers Grimm wrote about 200 fairy tales. [2]In these stories males and females are not exactly equal. [3]Sixteen wicked mothers or stepmothers exist, and only three wicked fathers or stepfathers. [4]There are twenty-three evil female witches and only two evil male witches. [5]Included in the stories are thirteen young women who endanger men and only one man that harms his bride. (Combine into two sentences.)

**a.** Combine sentences 1 and 2.

**b.** Revise sentences 3, 4, and 5, using parallel structure. Start the sentence with "There are..."

*Your rewrite:*_____

_____

_____

_____

_____

_____

_____

_____

_____

_____

# 40

## COMBINING SENTENCES
## USE THEM IN <u>YOUR</u> WRITING!

On an otherwise sunny morning, you walk into English class and find yourself presented with an unexpected essay test. You are asked to write a report or essay of about 200 words on one of four topics. The sun disappears, and the day is instantly grey and miserable ... as you look at the four topics.

(a) an accident
(b) a biography of a famous person
(c) a performance
(d) a visit to a city

Do they sound dull? They *are* dull! Part of your job, as a writer, is to make them exciting! Here's how ...

*Step 1:* Choose one of the four topics.

Consider "a." Do you remember a particularly horrifying accident? Or an amusing one? This is a "possible" for almost everyone.

Consider "b." Do you know a great deal about a pop singer, or a baseball player, or some other well-known person? If you do, you may want to try working with this topic. If you don't, draw a line through "b"—and forget it.

Consider "c." Have you seen a movie, or a TV program, a play or a concert that particularly impressed you? Do you remember it clearly? If your answer is *yes*, you may want to choose this topic. If your answer is *no*, draw a line through it.

Consider "d." Have you visited an interesting city recently? Is your own city interesting enough to attract an out-of-town visitor. Decide if this topic is possible—for *you*.

Make a decision. Ask yourself which topic you know the most about ... which topic interests you most. Then choose.

*Step 2:* Next, *angle* your topic. This means—narrow it; take a particular attitude toward it.

EXAMPLES:

(a) Writing about accidents can be boring. Choose a particular accident. Then angle it. Perhaps—"Speeding can be dangerous to your health—as three teenagers found out at a railway crossing."

(b) Choose a famous person you know a great deal about. Then find an angle. Explain *why* Jesse Owens will never be forgotten as long as the Olympics are held—or *how* Michael Jackson's life-style influenced his young audiences.

(c) Think of a performance you will never forget. Ask yourself: *why* was this performance unforgettable? Was it a particular actor? The setting? Special sound effects? Any of these could suggest an angle.

(d) Choose a city—and angle your approach. "Washington, D.C.—the Political City" or "Behind the Scenes in Hollywood, California" or "*My* City: Why Tourists Come Here" (or even, Why Tourists *Don't* Come Here!).

Choose the angle for your topic. Write it below.

_____

*Step 3:* You now have a topic and an angle. Jot down any details that will help you to develop that angle.

_____

_____

_____

_____

_____

*Step 4:* Decide how you are going to organize your essay: from a generalization to details, or from details to a generalization? Categorically, spatially, or chronologically? Which?

_____

*Step 5:* Write your essay on scrap paper, keeping your angle firmly in mind.

*Step 6:* Revise your essay. Remember the various techniques you have been studying and *use* them. If your sentences are short and choppy, do some sentence combining.

*Step 7:* Copy the final draft of your essay below.

_____

_____

_____

_____

_____

_____

_____

_____

_____

_____

_____

_____

_____

_____

_____

_____

_____

_____

_____

_____

_____

_____

_____

Any time you are asked to write a report or essay about one of several topics, use this procedure. It will simplify your life ... and make *you* a better writer!

*WRITING TECHNIQUE*

# 13 ━━━━━━━━━━

**Last but not least—sentence combining. With it, your writing will be smooth yet varied, mature yet interesting. Use this technique frequently—as you proceed along the road to better writing ...**

# WRITING TIME—IV

Below is a paragraph about Sean on the last day of school. It contains a good deal of information, but this information is given in a series of short, dull sentences. Your job: rewrite the paragraph completely. Make it come alive. Make the reader feel Sean's sense of freedom. Make the reader *see* and *smell* and *hear*. Do all this by remembering and using the various writing techniques you have been practicing.

> Sean put his books in the closet. Sean is twelve years old. School was over. For ten weeks he was free. He could go to the movies. He could go surfing. He could go swimming. He could lie in the grass and just dream. He could run. He could leap. He could climb trees. He had ten weeks of freedom.

YOUR REVISION:

_____

_____

_____

_____

_____

_____

Are you pleased with your rewrite? Swap papers with a few classmates and see how different people approached the rewriting in different ways.

Now take back your own paper and try one more rewrite. This time keep as much of your own version as you can, but change "Sean" to "I"—in other words, write the paragraph from a first-person point of view. You may have to change a few words here and there as you change pronouns. Write your second version below.

_____

_____

_____

_____

_____

Which do you like better: your first rewrite or your second? Why?

_____

_____

_____

You see? You are not only becoming a better writer; you are also becoming your own editor!

**B. WRITING TIME**

Have you ever heard of Sidewalk Sam? Read the following *true* information about him . . . .

Sidewalk Sam is a sidewalk artist.

His real name is Bob Guillemin.

His paintings have been exhibited in museums all over the country.

He uses chalk for his sidewalk drawings.

In December, 1982, he drew the Mona Lisa on the sidewalk of West 43rd Street, New York City.

As a background for the Mona Lisa, he used three Miami Beach hotels: the Doral, the Eden Roc, and the Fountainebleau Hilton.

These three hotels commissioned the painting.

Sidewalk Sam also recreates other masterpieces on sidewalks.

He has recreated paintings by Rembrandt, Van Gogh, and Vermeer.

Said Sidewalk Sam: "You should see my Vermeer. You wouldn't think Vermeer would look good with bubble gum and cracks."

Said Sidewalk Sam: "I have a goal. Someday I am going to do the Sistine Chapel ceiling on the ground."

1.  Play the reporter. Use the above information to write a brief, amusing feature story for your school newspaper. Remember that your audience will be made up of people *your* age. Write for *them*.

_____

_____

_____

_____

_____

_____

[*continued*]

_____

_____

_____

_____

_____

_____

_____

_____

_____

_____

_____

_____

2. Now read your story. Did you use different kinds of sentences? Are some sentences short, some long? Are your verbs dramatic and your nouns specific? Have you used a few sharp, graphic adjectives and adverbs? Revise. Replace. Add. Delete. Then copy your revised story below.

_____

_____

_____

_____

_____

_____

_____

_____

_____

_____

_____

_____

_____

_____

_____

_____

_____

Andy Rooney, the newspaper columnist, once wrote an article about his "favorites and least favorites" in fifteen categories. One category was **food.** Rooney wrote a brief paragraph mentioning that his favorites were rice and ice cream and that, in his family, they cooked rice in a hundred different ways. He ended the paragraph with two short sentences: "I don't want to talk about ice cream. It's made me what I am today, over 200 pounds."

Notice the quiet touch of humor in that last sentence.

Rooney then went on to describe his "least favorites" in the **food** category.

> I dislike anything made with gelatin, including Jell-O. Veal and turnips are not on the menu if I have anything to do with planning it, either.

Notice the participle "including" modifying "gelatin." And the gerund "planning" used as object of the preposition "with." But notice especially that Rooney's style is casual—almost as though he were in the same room speaking with the reader.

Your assignment? To write a newspaper column of your own, dealing with your favorites and least favorites in *five* different categories. Some possible categories (but you may develop your own if you like):

| | | |
|---|---|---|
| **Foods** | **Colors** | **Cars** |
| **Clothing** | **Numbers** | **Chores** |
| **Athletes** | **Weather** | **Activities** |
| **Beverages** | **School Subjects** | **Stores** |

*Procedure:*  (work on scrap paper)

**1.** Write a brief introduction—perhaps two sentences. Make it interesting and provocative.

**2.** Select *five* categories. For each one, write one paragraph about your favorites and one paragraph about your least favorites. Keep your style like Andy Rooney's: casual, light, and (if possible) humorous.

**3.** Revise everything you have written. Check your use of all *thirteen* writing techniques.

| | |
|---|---|
| 1. Specific nouns | 7. Four types of sentences |
| 2. Specific verbs | 8. Compound sentences |
| 3. Apt adjectives | 9. Complex sentences |
| 4. Agile adverbs | 10. Appositives |
| 5. Personal pronouns | 11. Parallel structures |
| 6. Purposeful prepositions | 12. Verbals |

—and, of course,—

13. Combining Sentences.

**229**

Work on your revision until your writing is as polished, as smooth as you can make it. Then add a title (try alliteration or rhyme) and copy the completed column below.

> "But words are things, and a small drop of ink
> Falling like dew upon a thought, produces
> That which makes thousands, perhaps millions, think.
> Byron. *Don Juan*

_____

_____

_____

_____

_____

_____

_____

_____

_____

_____

_____

_____

_____

_____

_____

_____

_____

_____

_____

_____

_____

_____

_____

_____

_____

_____

[*continued*]

_____

_____

_____

_____

_____

_____

_____

_____

_____

_____

_____

_____

_____

_____

_____

_____

_____

_____

_____

_____

_____

_____

_____

_____

_____

Is your column easy to read? Is it always interesting? Is it smooth and easy to understand? If you can answer **yes** to all three questions, you have mastered the *thirteen basic techniques of better writing* ... Congratulations!

# "Put It All Together ... "

You have mastered thirteen techniques: thirteen steps to better writing. Now what?

**Now**—you really write! You take all you have learned and you move ahead. You take dozens of seemingly unrelated facts and you organize them. You think about them. You find you have something unique and fascinating to say. And you say it ... effectively, skillfully, well.

It's a little like learning to be a cook. First you learn the techniques: how to cream butter, how to beat an egg, how to saute and broil and knead. But the fun comes when you *put it all together:* when you cook a delicious dinner or bake a fabulous cake.

It's a little like learning to be a carpenter. First you learn the techniques: how to hammer a nail straight, how to saw wood, how to measure and sand and polish. But the fun comes when you *put it all together:* when you make a broken chair whole again, or when you build a small but elegant table.

*You* have learned the techniques of writing—and you're ready for the fun part. You're ready to *put it all together*.

To help you, we have assembled three portfolios, each dealing with a topic almost guaranteed to interest you—

> **Snakes ...**
> **Names ...** and
> **Movies** (with emphasis on *special effects*)

Each portfolio starts with two pages of fascinating facts. Your job is to use the thirteen techniques to turn these facts into sharp, effective letters and reports, essays and stories.

Are you ready?

# PORTFOLIO I—SNAKES

... What animal do you most dislike? Twelve thousand children in the British Isles were asked that question. To no one's great surprise, the "winner" was the snake—named by 27% of the children. (1)

... Snakes can't close their eyes—ever. They can contract their pupils a bit, but their eyes are always open and glittering. (2)

... Two thousand years ago snake fat was used to prevent baldness. (3)

... Snakes can be quite long: the python, about 33 feet; the anaconda, about 28 feet. (4)

... In the 19th century in the U.S., rattlesnake oil was used to treat rheumatism, sore eyes, deafness, ringworm, tumors, and toothache. (5)

... Snakes are usually bought and sold by the *foot*. The longer the snake, the bigger the price per foot. Recently good-sized snakes were selling for $20 to $30 per foot. (6)

... Keeping a snake as a pet is fairly expensive. They must be fed freshly killed (or living) mice, guinea pigs, rats, or rabbits. (7)

... In ancient Greece, Aesculapius, the god of medicine, carried a snake staff. Today a staff, twined with two snakes and called a *caduceus*, is the emblem of physicians. (8)

... Snake skins, ground into powder, have been used to treat sore throats, cramps, backaches, and sprains. Boiled in wine, it was considered good for earache and colic. (9)

... According to some old folklore tales, anyone who ate the boiled flesh of a white snake thereby acquired all medical knowledge. (10)

... Several times a year a snake sheds its skin. The snake rubs its face against a rough object until it breaks the skin near the lips. It then moves *forward* out of the skin, leaving behind the entire old skin turned inside out. As a result, people once thought snakes were immortal—that they lived forever. (11)

... In China the flesh of the boa was once used to fight tuberculosis. (12)

... Snakes live to be twenty years old, occasionally more. (13)

... The rattlesnake shakes its rattles to warn away any approaching attacker. Some snakes hiss for the same reason. (14)

... Sea snakes were once considered effective against malaria and epilepsy. (15)

... Most snakes reproduce by laying eggs. Baby snakes bite their way out of the eggs and are immediately on their own. (16)

... Snake flesh is eaten throughout the world. It is said to taste like chicken, or eel, or veal, or frog. At gourmet centers today, one can buy canned rattlesnake or rattlesnake soup. (17)

... In temperate regions, many snakes hibernate in winter. Sometimes thousands curl up in the same cave to keep warm. (18)

... Snakes have been used in warehouses, as exterminators of rodents. (19)

... In the Middle Ages, barrels of snakes were sometimes thrown over the walls of a besieged town. The snakes threw the inhabitants into panic and led to their surrender. (20)

... Snake charmers have long been popular. As they play a flute, the snake, seemingly enchanted, moves rhythmically. Actually all snakes are deaf, and the snake would react in the same way to a moving stick. (21)

... Hannibal once ordered that pots filled with snakes be tossed into enemy ships. The Romans quickly surrendered. (22)

... In Brazil it was once believed that if you took a rattle from a rattlesnake's tail and put it inside your guitar, the tone of the instrument would improve and so would the singer's voice. (23)

... In the U.S., if you see "prairie eel" on a menu, be warned: it is another name for rattlesnake. (24)

... Snakes are *not* slimy. They are actually dry and quite pleasant to the touch. (25)

... In ancient Egypt and Rome, snakes were kept as household pets. In fact, owning a snake was quite a status symbol. (26)

... The Hopi Indians in Arizona still perform the annual Rain Dance. Beautifully costumed priests hold rattlers between their teeth and dance fiercely. Later they release the snakes on a plateau. It is believed the snakes quickly disappear into holes in the ground where they pass on the rain prayers to the gods of the underworld. (27)

... In the Bible, it was a snake that tempted Eve to eat the forbidden fruit. Since then, the snake has often been considered a symbol of evil. (28)

... Snakes sometimes poison people— but more often people poison snakes. Insects killed by insecticides are eaten by snakes. The insecticides accumulate in the liver and the liver swells, causing death. (29)

... Snake skins are tough and durable and completely waterproof. They are used to make handbags, shoes, belts, ties, and chair covers. (30)

... Cobras were once worshipped in India, and pythons in Africa. In Australia, the bushmen considered snakes as water-gods, necessary to make rainfall or to find springs. (31)

... In the 18th century, some Colonial flags carried a picture of a rattlesnake and the motto: "Don't tread on me." The rattler was a favorite U.S. symbol because, "like the segments of the rattlesnake's tail, the Colonies were independent yet firmly united." (32)

... Quetzalcoatl of Mexico was a famous feathered serpent: a combination of bird and snake. It was the god of civilization. After its reign, it set sail in a boat made of snakeskin. Years later, when the Spaniards arrived in their shining armor, the Aztecs thought Quetzalcoatl had returned and welcomed the invaders. (33)

... A legendary snake, the Mindi of Australia, was believed to be ten miles long with a huge head and a three-pronged tongue. It was said to cause smallpox epidemics. (34)

... A snake is sometimes called a serpent or a reptile. A road that winds like a snake is described as "serpentine." (35)

... Snake sayings:
   "He's a snake in the grass."
      (a betrayer, a false friend)
   "Put a snake in your bosom, and it will sting when it is warm."
      (proverb) (36)

# 1. FINDING ANSWERS

Snakes are fascinating! Learn a little about these intriguing creatures by reading the 36 items in Portfolio I (pages 233–234). Then return to this page.

\* \* \* \* \* \* \*

Now that you are an expert on snakes, use the 36 items to find some answers.

1. How do insecticides kill snakes as well as insects?

_____

_____

2. About how much would you pay for a six-foot snake? (You'll need a little math to answer this one!)

_____

3. You have been asked to write a report about the various ways snakes have been used throughout history. List below (by number) *all* the items that contain *relevant* (related) information. (The number of each item appears at the end of the item.)

_____

4. You have been asked to write a report about the relationship between snakes and religion throughout history. List below (by number) *all* items that contain *relevant* information.

_____

5. You have been asked to write a report about snakes and war. List below (by number) *all* items that contain *relevant* information.

_____

6. You have been asked to write a report about snakes as pets. List below (by number) *all* items that contain *relevant* information.

_____

# 2.  WRITING A REPORT

Writing a report—whether for school or for work—is not very difficult if you remember three basic procedures:

> *select* relevant material,
> *organize* the material logically,
> *write* in a clear, interesting style.

You have already completed the first procedure for four different reports: see page 235. From exercises 3, 4, and 5, select one report you would like to write. (We will deal with exercise 6 in the next chapter.)

> Uses of Snakes
> Snakes and Religion
> Snakes and War

Your choice:_____

*First Step:*  Reread the items you selected so that the relevant material is fresh. Think about it for a minute. Select a working title: something that explains what you are writing about *and* catches a reader's interest. For example, for a report about Snakes and War, a possible title would be "Don't Tread on Me!" Choose a title and write it on the top line of page 238.

*Second Step:*  Write a sparkling introductory paragraph of about two sentences. You may wish to begin with a rhetorical question or a quotation or with some other writing technique.

EXAMPLE:  "Don't tread on me!" shouted the Colonists in 1776, warning England that—like a rattler—they would strike back if attacked. Throughout history, the snake has been used in war to create panic and terror in the hearts of even the bravest opponents.

EXAMPLE:  Which animal is most disliked? The answer—to no one's surprise—is the snake. Yet throughout history the snake has contributed to human welfare and has helped to stuff human wallets and bankbooks.

*Your turn.*  Remember your topic and your title. Select an idea, a question, or a quotation that will work for you and write a brief introductory paragraph. Work on scrap paper. When you are satisfied with it, copy it on page 238.

*Third Step:* Examine once more the items you selected from Portfolio I. Combine them into clusters. (For example, all *medical* uses of snakes may be combined into one cluster.) Try to end with *three* clusters. Next decide in what order you wish to use these clusters, or categories. Write the order below, by listing appropriate numbers.

Category 1: _____

Category 2: _____

Category 3: _____

*Fourth Step:* Take the category you listed first. Write a paragraph using the relevant material. Work on scrap paper.

*Fifth Step:* Take the category you listed second. Write a paragraph using the relevant material.

*Sixth Step:* Take the category you listed third. Write a paragraph using the relevant material.

> Steps 4, 5, and 6 will form the *body* of your report. These paragraphs should be chockful of information—but also, of course, should be well-written, interesting, possibly even amusing.

*Seventh Step:* Check steps 4, 5, and 6 now. Revise. Think about the writing techniques you have been learning. Are the sentences of various types and lengths? Are the verbs action-packed? Are the nouns specific, the adjectives and adverbs apt? Examine your paragraphs with a critical eye and make any changes that seem desirable. Copy them—*after revision—* onto page 238.

*Eighth Step:* Everything needs a conclusion: a cake needs icing, an election needs a winner. And a report needs a conclusion. It should be closely related to the report as a whole, and it should leave the reader with a new idea, or with a question to be pursued.

EXAMPLE: Slithering through the grass, eyes wide open and glittering, the snake remains today what it has been through the centuries: a symbol of good or a symbol of evil; a god or a devil; but always—the object of human fascination.

*Your turn.* Write a good concluding paragraph; revise it; and copy it on the next page.

\*    \*    \*    \*    \*    \*

There you have it! A complete report—a well-written essay, a joy to read and a joy to have written! Well—it is, isn't it? Best of all, you can use the same procedure again and again to write *any* report ... whether about **Snakes** or **Space**, or **Slippery Sergeants**!

# 3. WRITING A FRIENDLY LETTER

Do research to write a friendly letter? Of course. Doesn't everyone?

Suppose ... a friend of yours who lives halfway across the country tells you he's thinking of buying a twenty-foot python and keeping it as a pet. You're a mini-expert on snakes now, aren't you? You're a friend, aren't you? So write a letter ...

> ... congratulating him on selecting such an unusual pet
>
> **or**
>
> ... berating him for choosing such a dangerous pet.

*Don't* let yourself slip into generalities, repeating over and over how wonderful (or how terrible) a snake would be as a pet. *Do* use your relevant information about snakes to persuade him that he is right—or wrong.

On page 235, exercise #6, you selected some relevant items about snakes as pets. Start there.

1. Decide which you will do: persuade your friend to go ahead and buy a python; or persuade him to try a poodle instead.

2. Organize your information, numbering each item—or cluster of items—in the order in which you will use them.

3. Then write. Since this is a friendly letter, keep your style casual and informal. *And*—be persuasive.

Work on scrap paper first. Then revise—keeping in mind the various writing techniques you have been learning. Make the letter interesting—and amusing—and helpful. When you have finished, copy the final draft on the next page.

_____(date)

Dear_____,

    So you're going to keep a twenty-foot python as a pet! I must say you are_____

_____

_____

_____

_____

_____

_____

_____

_____

_____

_____

_____

_____

_____

_____

_____

_____

                        _____ (As ever, or Your friend)

                        _____ (*your* first name)

# 4. WRITING A FABLE

Once upon a time there was a clever snake that admired its own cleverness immensely. "No one can hoodwink me!" he bragged. "I keep my eyes open *all* the time!" One night a squadron of small gray mice danced enticingly just out of reach. He watched, eyes glittering, as he pondered the best way to catch all of them at once. While he was pondering, strong hands grasped his tail and thrust him into a heavy canvas sack. He was toted off to a zoo where he spent the rest of his life examining his supposed cleverness. Moral: even when your eyes are open, your rear may be unprotected.

A *fable* is a short, short story in which the main characters are animals. Its purpose is to teach a moral lesson—a moral lesson that is applicable to humans. The above fable teaches us that a hoodlum, for example, intent on mugging some old people, may forget to guard his rear and may find himself nabbed by the police.

Because a fable is so short, it is extremely important to write skillfully: to use dramatic verbs, nouns, adverbs, and adjectives, and to pack each sentence with information and action.

Your turn. Think about snakes. Select one quality or characteristic of snakes that you can use as the focal point for a fable. Then create a little story around that focal point—and be sure your fable ends with a *moral*.

Work on scrap paper.

Revise.

Copy the final draft below.

_____

_____

_____

_____

_____

_____

_____

_____

_____

_____

_____

_____

_____

_____

# PORTFOLIO II—NAMES

... A few years ago women insisted that hurricanes no longer be named only for women. Now male and female names alternate—so Hurricane Alfred may be followed by Barbara, by Craig, by Dora, etc. (1)

..."As his name is, so is he." *(Bible. Samuel.)* (2)

...Boys with unusual names are more likely to commit crimes or to suffer from nervous disorders, according to several studies. Girls, however, like unusual names and are most likely to be unhappy if they consider their names too common. (3)

...Car manufacturers spend much time and money to find the right name for a new car. Most popular: names of birds—Eagle, Thunderbird, Skyhawk; and names of weapons—Cutlass, Javelin, Dart, LeSabre. Unpopular: the Chevy Nova in Puerto Rico where "no va" means "does not go." (4)

...Harvey is often considered a dull name. In 1979, the Harveys of the world (including Harvey van Cliburn, the pianist) banded together to erase this attitude and convince people that Harveys are charming and suave. (5)

...People with last names that begin with the letters A through R live about twelve years longer than do people whose last names begin with the letters S through Z. They are also healthier, less prone to ulcers, coronaries, and neuroses. (6)

...Some years ago the St. Regis Paper Company, which makes grocery bags, found that six percent of their bags were defective. They had machine operators put their names rather than numbers on the bags they made. The number of defective bags immediately dropped to less than one percent. (7)

...Tommy Wilson was timid and insecure, a proper Mother's boy, who often suffered from indigestion and headaches. When he was 24, Tommy proposed to his cousin and was rejected...and decided it was time for a change. He bought a new wardrobe, grew sideburns, and dropped his first name in favor of his middle name. He became—Woodrow Wilson, 28th President of the United States. (8)

...Burl Ives was born Burl Icle Ivanhoe; Roy Rogers was Leonard Slye; Twiggy was Lesley Hornby; and Mickey Rooney and Judy Garland were Joe Yule and Frances Gumm. (9)

...A nursery rhyme...
Monday's child is fair of face,
Tuesday's child is full of grace,
Wednesday's child is full of woe,
Thursday's child has far to go.
Friday's child is loving and giving,
Saturday's child works hard for a living.
But the child that is born on the Sabbath Day,
Is bonny and blithe and good and gay.
(10)

...Centuries ago the Egyptians and the aboriginal Australians and some American Indians kept their true names secret. They believed that letting outsiders possess their names gave the outsiders power over them. (11)

...A young woman, thinking of getting married, scribbles her future new name to see how her own first name combines with her young man's surname. (12)

...CB names tend to be a bit weird: Silver Fox, Rubber Duck, Granny GoGo, and Mule Skinner, for example. (13)

...The Ashantis of Ghana name their children after the day of the week on which they are born. Children born on Wednesday are believed to be moody and aggressive. Wednesday boys are more often arrested by juvenile authorities than other boys. (14)

...Why do people name their children as they do? Some name their children after relatives; some choose a name that sounds well with the surname; some name their children after film stars or other celebrities. (15)

...Naming racehorses is difficult since all names must abide by dozens of rules and be approved by the Jockey Club. No book or movie titles are allowed—no trade names—no abbreviations. One owner chose names that began with "Aff"—like Affectionately and Affiliate. Other interesting monikers: Over and Out, Watergate Era, Stop the Press. (16)

...TV talk show hosts go in for nicknames...note Johnny Carson, Mike Douglas, Phil Donahue, Dick Cavett, and Merv Griffin. (17)

...Parents (and sometimes teachers) when annoyed with a child will turn formal. "Robert," they say, instead of "Bob." "Victoria," they chide, instead of "Vicki." (18)

...Hiram Ulysses Grant was incorrectly enrolled in West Point as Ulysses Simpson Grant. (Simpson was his mother's maiden name.) That gave the future Civil War general the useful signature *U.S.* Grant—certainly helpful when he ran for President of the *U.S.* (19)

...Schizophrenics frequently forget their names or deliberately choose new ones. A favorite choice is "God." (20)

...When a person becomes *really* famous, he or she is often known by only one name: to wit, Bing (Crosby), Liz (Taylor), Lucille (Ball), Brando (Marlon), and Hepburn (Kate). (21)

...Today many women, especially career women, keep their own names even after marriage. Sometimes they use their maiden name as a middle name. Sometimes the couple keeps both last names, hyphenated: Syl and Jack Ogden-Brown. (22)

...Famous nicknames of the famous:
  Honest Abe—Abraham Lincoln
  Schnozzola—Jimmy Durante
  Ringlets—Gen. George Custer
  Stonewall—Andrew Jackson
  Long Tom—Thomas Jefferson
  Duke—John Wayne (23)

...**Surname**: last name or family name. (24)

...Odd names can be a liability when you are in school but an asset if you become an executive. Consider *Rawleigh* Warner (Mobil Oil); *Willibald* H. Conzen (Schering-Plough); and *Derald* H. Ruttenberg (Studebaker-Worthington). (25)

...Cherokee and Arapaho Indians and some Eskimos allow people to take new names at different stages of their life. (26)

...You can change your name, but you can also modify it. If your name is Charles Edward Brown, you can be...
  Charles E. Brown
  C. Edward Brown
  C. E. Brown
  C. Edward-Brown
...or even Chuck E. Brown, if you decide to become a comic! (27)

...Charles Manson immediately renamed new members to his California cult. This act weakened their sense of self-identity. Kidnappers of Patty Hearst changed her name to Tania probably for the same reason. (28)

...People with S-Z last names have a tough time because they are always *waiting*. They're the last to receive school grades, the last to be called on, the last in line. (29)

# 5. WRITING A FILLER

A *filler* is a short, interesting item (about 100 words) used to fill a hole in newspaper or magazine text. It should be informative, well-written, and—if possible—amusing.

First read the filler to the right. Notice that it combines items 6 and 29 (from Portfolio II). It opens with a rhetorical question that should "catch" most readers. It closes with a quotation that is familiar to just about everyone.

> Is your last name *Adams*—or *Smith*? If it's Adams, you will probably live twelve years longer than poor old Smith! Why? Because people whose last names begin with A through R are healthier than people whose last names begin with S through Z. They not only are physically healthier (fewer ulcers and coronaries, for example); they also are mentally healthier, with fewer neuroses. The unlucky S-Zs are always waiting—waiting to be called on, waiting for Social Security checks, waiting for tickets to a rock concert. And all that waiting is "dangerous to your health"!

Now it's your turn to write a filler...about **nicknames.**

1. Browse through Portfolio II and select any material relevant to the topic, nicknames. Make notes below.

_____

_____

_____

_____

_____

_____

2. Think about nicknames. Maybe you have one. Maybe some of your friends do. Maybe you know a few that belong to sports personalities or rock stars. Make notes below.

_____

_____

_____

_____

_____

**3.** Organize. Reread your material. Find a hook, an angle. For example: Do nicknames reflect physical characteristics? Are they amusing or hurtful? Why do some people receive nicknames, while others do not? Think. Decide what your angle will be and describe it briefly.

_____

_____

**4.** You're ready to begin writing. Keep your angle firmly in mind and start to write (on scrap paper). When you have finished, revise— remembering your thirteen writing techniques. Then copy the final draft below.

_____

_____

_____

_____

_____

_____

_____

_____

_____

_____

_____

_____

_____

_____

_____

_____

_____

_____

If you are pleased with your filler, you may want to submit it to your school newspaper. Imagine something *you* have written—*in print*!

# 6.   WRITING A BOOK

Yes—that title is a bit of an exaggeration. But with a little effort, you and your classmates *can* write a brief and interesting booklet about **names**. Here's how.

**A.**   Start with your own name. (If two of you in the same class have the same name, you may wish to work together.) Write your first name below.

_____

**B.**   List celebrities, past and present, with the same first name. Think of politicians, athletes, entertainers. List as many as you can. Identify each one briefly.

_____

_____

_____

_____

**C.**   Do a little research. Check the catalog in your school library. Are there any books about names? If there are, you will probably find a section in it about first names and their meanings. (An especially useful book is *The Name Game* by Christopher P. Andersen.) Find the meaning of *your* name and write it below.

_____

**D.**   Are there any common nicknames that derive from your first name? List them.

_____

**E.**   Can you think of any fictional characters that share your first name? Think of the books you have read—the TV shows you have seen—movies—songs—folklore or legendary tales. List and describe each such character briefly.

_____

_____

_____

**F.**   Take a poll. Ask a few people what they think of when they hear certain names. Mention a couple of names (perhaps *Dorothy* and *Timothy*) *and* your own first name. Write the results of the poll below.

_____

_____

_____

_____

**G.** Consider the physical structure of your first name.

   **1.** Is it one-syllable, two, or more? (*Kirk* is one syllable; *El len* is two; *Jon a than* is three.) How many syllables are in your name?_____

   **2.** Does it have a hard or soft sound? (*Kirk* is hard, with the two "k"s. *Sally* is soft, with the soft "s" and "l"s.) Which is yours?_____

   **3.** Are there any words that rhyme well with your name? (*Kirk* rhymes with "perk" or "jerk" or "lurk.") Or are there any that rhyme with a shortened form of your first name? (*Dot* rhymes with "hot" and "not" and "lot.") List some, if possible.

   _____

   **4.** How many letters are in your name?_____

**H.** *Why* were you given your first name? Were you named after a relative? After a celebrity? Check with your parents. If you can find the reason, write it below.

   _____

   _____

**I.** You now have oodles of information about your first name. **Think!** Find a good angle and use it in a good opening sentence (or sentences).

   EXAMPLE:  Thomases are terrific! Think of Tom Jefferson and Tom Jones and the shrewd and mischievous Tom Sawyer. For that matter, think of me...

   EXAMPLE:  "I dream of Jeannie with the light brown hair," wrote Stephen Foster, and I like to believe that, in some magical way, he was writing about me!

   Your turn...

   _____

   _____

   _____

   _____

**J.** Last step: Take your opening sentence(s) (written in item I above) and develop it, using any of the material you collected in steps A through H. Work on scrap paper. Revise your writing until it gleams! Then copy it on the next page.

_____

_____

_____

_____

_____

_____

_____

_____

_____

_____

_____

_____

_____

_____

_____

_____

_____

_____

_____

_____

If you and your classmates are interested. . .

- collect the best of the results (or all of them)
- persuade someone to type them
- make photostatic copies
- staple pages together—and—presto

**You have a book all your own!**

Save it. Years from now you will reread it with delight!

# 7. WRITING A FRIENDLY LETTER

A relative or a friend just had a baby. It's a _____ (boy or girl—you decide). The parents of the baby are uncertain as to what name to choose. Write a letter urging your relative or friend to choose a specific name or particular type of name. Before you make your decision, reread Portfolio II and make notes of any information that supports your point of view. (See page 240 for a review of format.)

Dear_____,

_____

_____

_____

_____

_____

_____

_____

_____

_____

_____

_____

_____

_____

_____ ,

_____

# 8. WRITING A REPORT

Write a report about **names** under the title...

### How Names Influence Our Lives

- Reread Portfolio II for *relevant* information.
- Probe your memory for more.
- Think about people and names you have read or heard about.
- Consider the people you know and their names.

When you have enough material...

think about it

organize it

write

revise...

...and, finally, copy the final draft of your report below.

_____

_____

_____

_____

_____

_____

_____

_____

_____

_____

*[continued]*

# PORTFOLIO III—MOVIES

... Need snow for a movie? One solution: grind up cornflakes and blow them through a machine. (1)

... When Cecil B. DeMille directed a film about a ship burning at sea, he simply had a tiny model placed in a tank of water. One problem remained: how to show people running frantically around the deck. Solution: paper figures of people were pasted on the backs of June bugs. When the boat was set on fire, the June bugs darted around desperately to get away from the flames. They looked *exactly* like people. (2)

... Stunt men and women get over $225 a day "just for showing up"—about $500 extra for taking a fifty-foot dive, and $1800 extra for letting themselves be set on fire. (3)

... Andy Warhol once said: "In the future there won't be any more stars. TV will be so accessible that *everybody* will be a star for fifteen minutes." (4)

... "Canned sound" can provide general laughter, children's laughter, applause, or even ball-crowd noises. Two fine comedy shows, "Mash" and "Barney Miller" were "sweetened" by having laughter added since they were filmed without an audience. On one of "The Beverly Hillbillies" programs, filmed with a live audience, the laughter was so enthusiastic that producers feared the TV audience wouldn't accept it. The real laughter was erased, and more moderate canned laughter was substituted. (5)

... Michael Landon and Burt Reynolds both started their careers as stuntmen. Hal Needham began as a stuntman, then became Burt Reynolds' double, and now directs films. (6)

... The pre-Inaugural galas of both Jimmy Carter and Ronald Reagan were "sweetened" by canned laughter and applause. (7)

... Kitty O'Neil, a well-known stuntwoman, has been deaf since infancy. She says that's a plus: she can concentrate better. A film was made about her: "Silent Danger." (8)

...Blood needed? No trouble in Hollywood. The actor simply keeps in his mouth a bit of red vegetable coloring and some cola until the moment he is "shot." Or—if body blood is needed, he holds a packet of technicolor blood to his body and crushes it when he is supposed to bleed. (9)

...On "The Little House on the Prairie," dresses had to *look* like homespun. What worked best was raw silk (at $12 to $16 a yard). Since about ten yards were needed, plus labor, Laura's simple little dresses cost a small fortune. (10)

...The show, "Real People," emphasizes the individuality and eccentricities of ordinary American citizens. A 17-year-old boy jumped rope 72 times in ten seconds. A Marine sergeant beeped "The Marines' Hymn" on a pocket calculator. Some middle-aged people in The Polar Bear Club jumped around on the beach and in the water of Lake George when the temperature was registering −9°. (11)

...The most serious injury that the stuntman Rick Baker ever suffered was a broken shoulder. He fell in a neighbor's living room while he was teaching some neighborhood kids how to fall safely. (12)

...King Kong, who made adults tremble and children shriek, was actually a rubber model just eighteen inches tall and weighing ten pounds. The dinosaurs in the same movie were also models. First the models were put into action against a suitable background and filmed. Then this film was projected on a big screen while the human actors went to work in front of it for the final filming. When King Kong holds Fay Wray, it's actually the *model* of Kong holding a *model* of Wray. (13)

...John Barbour, one of the hosts of "Real People," said: "In a time of confusion and frustration, the integrity of the single man or woman may be all we can cling to." (14)

...During fistfights on film, the punch never lands—it may miss by a dozen inches. But occasionally there's a slip-up and the stuntman ends up with a black eye. (15)

...When King Kong roared, what you were actually hearing was a lion's roar played backwards and at slower speed. (16)

...When Rick Baker worked as a stuntman on "The Towering Inferno," he wore an asbestos suit and had his face covered with masks and burn gel. Even so, he could withstand the flames only for about forty seconds. After that, human sweat turns to steam and burns even faster than fire. (17)

...To prevent injuries to stuntmen, bottles that are broken over someone's head are made of styrene plastic; and furniture that is to be broken over someone's head is made of balsa wood. (18)

...The stars themselves are not allowed to do any stunts that are dangerous. An injury can delay filming and cost hundreds of thousands of dollars. So stunt men and women are used in their places. (19)

...Many movies today are being made about "average" people: about the handicapped who have "made it"—about working mothers—about "ordinary" people who do extraordinary things. (20)

...Want to film a ship underway? First film the moving ocean—project this on a large screen and place the ship and actors in front of it. The illusion: that the ship is actually traveling. (21)

...An increasing number of TV shows are using the magazine format: a series of short "articles," some serious, some humorous. "Real People" is one example. "That's Incredible" is another. (22)

...In the movie *Earthquake*, Los Angeles was supposed to be almost totally destroyed. To achieve this effect, the director had sets built on heavy-duty springs that were moved by motors. In the same movie, when a dam breaks, some people are supposed to hack their way out of an underground garage. To simulate real concrete crumbling, the experts built a wall with a recipe containing a lot of sugar. "When the sugar hardened, it took days to drill through!" (23)

...In *Voyage to the Bottom of the Sea*, a movie, huge chunks of ice were to break off icebergs. These chunks were not ice at all—they were made with metal frames covered with wire mesh and then with wax-covered cheesecloth. (24)

# 9. WRITING A BUSINESS LETTER

You are a member of a group called "Future Moviemakers of America." You and your friends are interested in special effects: for example, how spaceships can be depicted as hurtling through space, and how weird-looking aliens can be used as the main characters in a movie.

Write a letter to A-to-Z Sci-Fi Studio (27 Ellington Road, Hollywood, California 12801) asking them if it would be possible for your group to borrow or rent a film about special effects. You know they have a film available: "All About Special Effects." (Name and address of the studio are fictitious.)

Work on scrap paper first. Be sure to include in your letter...

...the name of the film

...the fact you would like to borrow or rent it

...two or three special effects in which you are especially interested

...the name of your group and *why* you are interested in special effects.

On the next page is a sample *business* letter. Follow the format (position and punctuation of addresses, for example) *exactly*. And read the notes below.

Salutation (Dear Sir or Madam): Use a name, if possible; for example, Dear Mr. Edwards.

When you *handwrite* a letter, indent each paragraph.

Complementary closing (Very truly yours): this one or "Yours truly" is always safe in a business letter.

Signature: type or print your name *below* your signature.

SASE: an abbreviation meaning "*Self-a*ddressed *S*tamped *E*nvelope enclosed." (*Always* enclose a stamped, self-addressed envelope when you are asking for information or assistance.)

When you have finished your letter, revise it carefully, and copy it on page 256.

27 Owen Avenue
Bolton Landing, Iowa
June 22, 198__

R & C Zebra Studio
6161 Toll Road
Hollywood, California 12801

Dear Sir or Madam:

In the last few months several TV programs have been built on TV boners: flubbed lines, unplanned stumbles, and other oddities of filming. These shows are popular and appeal to viewers of all types.

I am a free-lance writer in the entertainment field and am planning to write a book about why actors make mistakes and why home audiences love to see them make mistakes. It is important that any information I use be accurate. Would it be possible for me to explore your library of discarded film cuttings and to talk with a few camera persons and/or editors?

Enclosed are some clippings from newspapers and magazines that will give you an idea of the work I have done in the past and of my professional skills. I hope you will agree to let me begin my research in the archives of your studio.

Very truly yours,

Janet D. Agee

SASE

# 10. WRITING A REPORT

You have already written reports about **snakes** and **names**. Now write one about **movies**. First—choose an angle. Some possibilities:

The World of Illusion (Special Effects)
Today Everybody's a TV Star
Stunts on Film

Next—reread Portfolio III for *relevant* information. Probe your memory for more.

Reread the suggested procedure for writing a report (pages 236–237).

**Think**. . .Organize your material. **Think**. . .Write. **Think**. . .Revise.

Copy the final draft of your report below.

_____

_____
_____
_____
_____
_____
_____
_____
_____

[*continued*]

# 11. WRITING A PERSUASIVE LETTER

You have already written a persuasive letter to a friend who was considering keeping a snake as a pet, and a second persuasive letter to a friend about naming a baby. Your skills should be sufficiently sharpened now so that you can tackle a most important type of persuasive letter: the Letter to the Editor.

*You* can make a difference when you write a sharp Letter to the Editor. If your letter is chockful of information, if it is written in an interesting, vital style, if it is provocative and/or amusing, you can change minds and behavior. You can become a leader, rather than a follower. You can become the one who makes things happen!

*Situation*:    You and several friends know a great deal about movie making. You decide it would be helpful to make a movie about your neighborhood, but you need a thousand dollars and the support of the public if you are to make a really good movie.

*Assignment*:    Write a Letter to the Editor. Include...

...*why* a movie about your neighborhood would help the people who live there.

...the kind of movie you envision—what you would be filming, etc.

...the estimated cost and how you hope to get the necessary backing.

...*how* the movie will be used after it is completed.

Before you begin writing, make careful notes for all four categories listed above (on scrap paper). Then organize and write. As you write, remember you are trying to *persuade* people to accept your ideas. Give them lots of information. Use a touch of alliteration to emphasize an important point. Use any of the writing techniques you have learned to give your letter *strength, power, impact*!

Copy the final draft on the following page.

_____
_____
_____
_____
_____
_____
_____
_____
_____
_____
_____
_____
_____
_____
_____
_____
_____
_____
_____
_____
_____
_____
_____
_____

**"You can make things happen
with a Letter to the Editor."**

# INDEX

adjective: 31–45, 47, 62, 63, 78, 98, 100, 116, 127, 151, 184, 195, 228, 229

ads: 34–35, 153

adverb: 49–63, 53–54 ("Tom Swifties"), 78, 97, 98, 116, 142, 143, 228, 229, 237

alliteration: 33–34, 259

angle: 62, 116, 224, 245, 246, 247, 249

answering questions: 235

appositive: 152–171, 204, 218, 219, 229

autobiography: 59–60

categorical organization: 113–117, 187–188, 207, 209, 229, 237, 259

chronological organization: 59–60, 61–62, 63, 99

clause
    independent: 134
    dependent: 134–137, 138–139, 140–141, 142, 204, 218, 220

combining sentences: 88–90, 92, 98, 124, 126–127, 128, 138–139, 141–143, 159–161, 163–164, 182, 184, 202–203, 204–205, 210–225, 229

comma: 124, 136, 163

comparison/contrast: 168, 169–171

complex sentence: 132–147, 151, 220, 229

compound object: 121, 122, 128

compound sentence: 118–131, 151, 220, 229

compound subject: 121, 122

compound verb: 121, 122, 141, 142

compound word: 120

conclusion, writing of: 47, 116, 189, 237

conjunction
    coordinate: 121–123, 125–126
    subordinate: 135–137, 138–141

declarative sentence: 102, 103, 107, 108–112, 114

dependent clause: 134–137, 138–139, 140–141, 142, 204, 218, 220

descriptive writing
    essays (see entries under **writing**)
    paragraphs (see entries under **writing**)
    sentences (see entries under **writing**)

details to generalization: 26–27, 28–29, 42–43, 144–145

details, use of: 3–4, 7–9, 12–15, 18–20, 80, 96–97, 148–149

diagramming: 85–86

dictionary, use of: 6, 21, 24, 37

exclamation point: 106

exclamatory sentence: 102, 106–107, 108–112, 114

expository writing
    essays (see entries under **writing**)

generalization to detail: 12–15, 30, 43, 44, 46–48, 144–145, 165, 166, 167, 206, 207

generalization to explanation: 128–131

gerund: 192, 193, 198–199, 204, 206, 229

imperative sentence: 102, 106, 107, **108,** 109, 110, 114

independent clause: 134

261

infinitive: 192, 193, 196–197, 204, 206

interrogative sentence: 102, 103–105, 108–112, 114, 128

introduction, writing of: 47, 62, 104, 105, 116, 188, 229, 236

letters (see entries under **writing**)

notetaking: 224, 235, 244, 246–247, 249, 250, 257

noun: 3–15, 23, 30, 38, 47, 62, 63, 78, 98, 100, 116, 126, 127, 142, 199, 228, 229

organization: 151, 176–178, 185–186, 224, 239, 245, 257
    categorical: 113–117, 187–188, 207, 209, 229, 237, 259
    chronological: 59–60, 61–62, 63, 99
    comparison/contrast: 168, 169–171
    details to generalization: 26–27, 28–29, 42–43, 144–145
    generalization to details: 12–15, 30, 43, 44, 46–48, 144–145, 165, 166, 167, 206, 207
    generalization to explanation: 128–131
    spatial: 75–76, 77–80, 209

outlining: 75, 77

paragraphs (see entries under **writing**)

parallel structure: 172–190, 220, 222, 229

participle: 192, 193–195, 200, 204, 206, 219, 229

parts of speech
    adjective (see separate entry)
    adverb (see separate entry)
    conjunction (see separate entry)
    noun (see separate entry)
    preposition (see separate entry)
    pronoun (see separate entry)
    verb (see separate entry)

persuasive writing
    essays (see entries under **writing**)
    letters (see entries under **writing**)
    paragraphs (see entries under **writing**)

point of view: 65, 69–74, 75–80, 226

poll, taking of: 246

preposition: 81–95, 98, 100, 204, 229

pronoun: 64–80, 226, 229

pun: 33–34

punctuation
    comma: 124, 136, 163
    exclamation point: 106
    question mark: 103–104
    quotation marks: 109

reference books
    dictionary: 6, 21, 24, 37
    thesaurus: 24
    synonyms, book of: 24

repetition: 56–57

revision (see entries under **writing**)

rhetorical question: 104–105, 109, 110, 114, 116, 236, 244

sentences (see entries under **writing**)

spatial organization: 75–76, 77–80, 209

story: (see entries under **writing**)

subordinate conjunction: 135–137, 138–141

synonyms: 24

thesaurus: 24

Tom Swifties: 53–54

verb: 16–30, 47, 62, 63, 78, 97, 98, 100, 116, 121, 122, 126, 127, 141, 142, 143, 146, 151, 183, 184, 228, 229, 237

verbals: 191–209, 229

vocabulary: 6, 21, 37

**words**
    compound: 120
    definitions: 6, 21, 37
    derivations: 157–158, 159
    lists: 5, 27, 78, 80, 98, 99, 127, 142

**writing**

### SENTENCES

general: 6, 21, 83–84, 87, 90–91, 93–94
appositives: 152–171, 204, 218, 219, 229
combining: 88–90, 92, 98, 124, 126–127, 128, 138–139, 141–143, 159–161, 163–164, 182, 184, 202–203, 204–205, 210–225, 229
complex: 132–147, 151, 220, 229
compound: 118–131, 151, 220, 229
declarative: 102, 103, 107, 108–112, 114
descriptive: 3, 4
details, use of: 3–4, 7–9, 12–15, 18–20, 80, 96–97, 148–149
exclamatory: 102, 106–107, 108–112, 114
four types of: 101–117, 184, 189, 228, 229, 237
gerund: 192, 193, 198–199, 204, 206, 229
imperative: 102, 106, 107, 109, 110, 114
infinitive: 192, 193, 196–197, 204, 206
interrogative: 102, 103–105, 108–112, 114, 128
parallel structure: 172–190, 220, 222, 229
participle: 192, 193–195, 200, 204, 206, 219, 229
point of view: 65, 69–74, 75–80, 226

### PARAGRAPHS

general: 93–95, 110, 111–112, 145, 150, 151
anecdote: 163–164
autobiographical: 59–60
categorical: 113–117, 187–188, 207, 209, 229, 237, 259

chronological: 59–60, 61–62, 63, 99
comparison/contrast: 168, 169–171
descriptive: 12–15, 26–27, 28–29, 42–43, 46–48, 185, 186, 206, 207, 208–209
details, use of: 12–15, 80, 148–149
details to generalization: 26–27, 28–29, 42–43, 144–145
explanations: 128–129, 129–130, 130–131
filler: 99, 128, 244–245
generalization to details: 12–15, 30, 43, 44, 46–48, 144–145, 165, 166, 167, 206, 207
revision of: 9–11, 24–25, 41, 56, 58, 72, 92, 98, 100, 126–127, 128–129, 141–143, 150, 151, 163–164, 182–183, 184, 204–205, 218–222, 226
sentence structure, varied: 108–110, 114–115, 116
spatial: 75–76, 77–80, 209
story: 63, 72, 151

### ESSAYS

general: 223–225, 227–228, 236–238, 246–248. 257–258
autobiographical: 229–231
categorical: 115–117, 187–188, 229–231, 237
descriptive: 46–48
expository: 250–251
generalization to details: 46–48
revision: 224, 228, 237, 247

### LETTERS

business: 254–256
friendly: 30, 44, 146–147
persuasive: 239–240, 249, 259–260

### STORIES

fable: 241
fish story: 63